THE BEST
MEN'S STAGE
MONOLOGUES
OF 1990

JOCELYN BEARD has edited <u>Contemporary Movie Monologues:
A Sourcebook for Actors</u> (Fawcett/Columbine, Spring 1991) and
<u>Comedy Monologues: A Sourcebook for Actors</u> (Fawcett/
Columbine, Winter 1991).

TERRY SCHREIBER is the founder and Artistic Director of the
Terry Schreiber Studio in New York City.

THE BEST
MEN'S STAGE
MONOLOGUES
OF 1990

Edited By
Jocelyn Beard

SK
A Smith and Kraus Book

A Smith and Kraus Book
Published by Smith and Kraus, Inc.

Library of Congress Catalog Card Number: 90-91798

ISBN: 0-9622722-2-1

Cover design by David Wise
Text design by Jeannette Champagne

Manufactured on recycled paper in the United States of America

First Edition: January 1991
10 9 8 7 6 5 4 3 2 1

Smith and Kraus, Inc.
Main Street, P.O. Box 10
Newbury, Vermont 05051
(802) 866-5423

Quality Printing and binding by Eagle Printing Co., Inc.
Albany, New York 12202, U.S.A

iv

ACKNOWLEDGMENTS

Grateful thanks to the playwrights for their extraordinary talent.

CONTENTS

CONTENTS

CONTENTS

ix

FOREWORD

When casting about for an appropriate adjective to assign the 1990 theatrical season, I kept returning to a simple, yet often exaggerated word: Fascinating.

This has certainly been a particularly fascinating year in theatre. Diverse offerings such as Craig Lucas' romantically eerie "Prelude To A Kiss" and Eric Bogosian's provocatively desolate "Sex, Drugs, Rock & Roll" are just examples of the intriguing mix of plays produced this season.

Tough issues like AIDS, torture and the homeless have been ardently tackled by this year's playwrights, creating a wealth of monologues that may be sampled in this book. The men's roles of this season represent a fantastic mix of types, from the opera-loving Mendy of "The Lisbon Traviata" by Terrence McNally to Augie, the terrible bully of José Rivera's "Each Day Dies With Sleep."

Fascinating.

1991 will have to go a long way to top this past season - but that's the great thing about show biz: You know it's going to do just that!

--Jocelyn Beard
Patterson, NY
August, 1990

INTRODUCTION

Recently, an intense young actor, auditioning for my studio, announced that he would perform a monologue from "The Glass Menagerie." Strike One. (This is material that any director can recite.) He then indulged in interminable preparation before finally beginning. Strike Two. He then paraphrased the entire speech. Strike Three.

I thanked the actor, and suggested that this would have been more suitable for a screen test than a stage presentation; and that he shouldn't paraphrase well known material. Considering his university major in drama, it was particularly off-putting that he would select an overdone speech and then rewrite it.

An example of how not to compensate for the lack of new audition material is gender-switching. A young woman once auditioned for me using a monologue of George's from "Who's Afraid of Virginia Woolf?"! (Disaster!) These anecdotes illustrate the actor's eternal quest: FINDING THE RIGHT MONOLOGUE.

The Best Men's Stage Monologues of 1990 responds to that quest. The editor has uncovered many fresh selections representing a tremendous variety of characters. Most importantly, the monologues make sense when taken out of context. The cuttings are all excellent choices, and although many of the plays may be unknown to directors, because of their newness, the monologues are fluid, logical and afford the actor an opportunity to present his best qualities. To a director, there is little so rewarding as an actor revealing himself, to great advantage, through the selection of appropriate material.

A monologue is a scene and should be rehearsed with the same demands: Who? What? When? Where? Why? Approaching the monologue as a scene will help the actor to overcome the justifiable fear of having to stand, "naked out there with all those words."

The actor's presentation of a monologue is frequently all a director can depend on for an initial evaluation of talent. It is therefore of paramount importance that the monologue material suit

INTRODUCTION

the specific qualities of the actor. In an initial meeting, I'm not interested in how the actor may be able to stretch. I am concerned, however, that what initially comes across is connected and emotionally truthful.

This book offers a great variety of essentially serious material. Nothing is more exciting than a new monologue performed by an actor who brings it to life, with total commitment to the material. This editor has really gone hunting. It is now up to you, the actor, to bring life to the playwrights' words.

Note To The Actor: Please read the full text upon which your monologue is based. Nothing is more disconcerting to me than to discover that the actor doesn't know what the play is about, in what context the speech occurs, or even who the author is! Also, please select something in your age range, avoid accents (unless requested), and above all choose a monologue that you really relate to either from personal experience or in your fertile imagination.

Remember, the audition is frequently as tense and uncomfortable for the director as it is for the actor. Directors are quite human, and tire at the end of a long day. You'll be way ahead of the game and generate interest with a selection that is new. When I cast a play I may initially request monologues rather than a scene from the play, and I sit up and take notice when the actor announces a play that I am not familiar with. New material insures that I will listen more intently than I will to standard line readings of tried and true material.

Buy the book - it's a good one - and go to work. Jocelyn Beard and Smith and Kraus Books have given you a great head start with the new material presented here. The rest is up to you.

--Terry Schreiber

THE BEST
MEN'S STAGE
MONOLOGUES
OF 1990

AMULETS AGAINST THE DRAGON FORCES
by Paul Zindel

Chris Boyd - 16 - Staten Island - 1955

Mrs. Boyd is a live-in nurse who has been hired by Mr. DiPardi to care for his dying mother. When Mrs. Boyd and her son, Chris, move into the DiPardi household, it soon becomes evident that nothing is as it seems. It seems that Mr. DiPardi is gay and has a thing for teen-age boys. Unknown to Mrs. Boyd, Chris is also gay. Mr. DiPardi feels that there is something familiar about Chris. When Mrs. DiPardi finally dies, the Boyd's prepare to leave. Chris stays behind a moment to tell Mr. DiPardi that they once spent the night together.

CHRIS: Mr. Dipardi--once you picked me up...Mr. DiPardi. About a year ago. I was hitchhiking on Richmond Terrace. I had been to the Empire Theater. You stopped in your Chevy, and I got in--your two-tone Chevy. You were drunk. You told me you owned a construction company. You said you had to stop by some offices. You took me to the brick building in front of your shipyard, and you told me to come inside with you because you had to make sure everything was locked up. You had a key for the front door. You locked the door behind us and took me into a back office. You got two bottles of beer from a small refrigerator and said we should sit down to drink them. I sat on a chair and you sat on a sofa. You leaned over the arm of the sofa. You were so drunk you had to put your beer down. You just looked at me. You didn't even talk. You held my hand. Finally, you fell asleep. I sat in the chair a long while with you holding my hand. Then I let myself out. *(Beat.)* Mr. DiPardi, I want to learn how to love...whoever I love...I don't want to be ashamed and angry like you. *(Chris gathers his bags and starts to leave.)*

1

APPLES
by Ian Dury

PC Honey - 20s-30s - London - Present

During a long day in court, a London bobby tells an overworked
Magistrate how he came to arrest a transvestite for disturbing the
peace.

PC HONEY: With your permission, ma'am, I have to inform the
court that the defendant standing in the dock, charged under the
name of Josephine McKenzie on one count of insulting behaviour
likely to cause a breach of the peace, two counts of indecent assault,
and fourteen counts of persistent aggravated public nuisance contrary
to paragraphs 97, 93 and 47 of the public order act of 1969, is in
actual fact a male person, one Arthur George Wallace, labourer, of
no permanent address, currently resident at the social services hostel
in Vauxhall, otherwise known as the marmite factory. At 8:45 last
night, the evening of the third of April, myself, PC Honey 739,
stationed at Kennington police station, was on street patrol duty in
the vicinity of Waterloo station when I received a call on my
personal receiver to proceed to the area of platform 19 on the main
concourse, where a woman had been reported creating a serious
disturbance at the entrance to the gentlemen's lavatories. I arrived
at 8:53 and took up a concealed position behind the Datsun car
display opposite platforms 16 and 17. From 8:54 until 9:32 I
observed the defendant's behaviour. He was wearing the same
headscarf and camelhair coat, and carrying the same leather handbag
that he is now, and I observed his making advances of a lewd and
suggestive nature on seventeen separate occasions to male travellers
entering the gents about their lawful business, on at least two of
which occasions he made actual physical contact with the said male
traveller's person, the second of which caused an immediate affray
upon which I left my place of concealment, and proceeded to caution
and subsequently arrest the defendant Wallace. At the time of the
arrest I did not realize that the defendant Wallace was a male person,
and before giving him into the charge of WPC Jones of Kennington
police station, I asked him to account for his unusual behaviour.
'You wouldn't understand Constable,' he said; 'it's me change.'

2

A QUIET END
by Robin Swados

Tony - 30s - New York City - Present
Tony, Max and Billy are AIDS patients who share an apartment on the upper west side of Manhattan. As they await the inevitable, they each reveal deep emotions concerning their lives and fates. Tony desired to be an actor, but the picture he paints of his experience with show business is filled with bitterness and regret.

TONY: Listen to me. I didn't give up on show business. I really gave it a shot. Sometime--I don't know when, exactly--I started to feel it slipping away from me. Like climbing the greasy pole at camp--remember? The way people's eyes would glaze over before I'd even answered their questions: "What have you done recently." "Be sure to let me know the next time you're in something." *(Pause.)* You know what my problem was? I couldn't handle the matinees. At the evening performances I was brilliant. I walked into the bars and I <u>had</u> those guys. I exploded in the dark. I could really turn it on, you know what I mean? If I was blind, it didn't matter. I had the lights to see for me. And if I was dead, I didn't know it. Nobody knew. Outside, where there's sun, and air, and people just living their lives, disco music's come and gone. But it's still there in the bars, beating away like an extra heart in case your own breaks down. And I never went home empty-handed. Ever. *(Pause.)* Fuckin' show business. Fifteen years ago they said, "You're too young." I said, "O.K., I've got time," and took another all-night tour of the bars. They <u>like</u> 'em young in the bars, I thought. And I was right. I felt like a failure if I went to bed before five. Three, four, five years go by...I'm pounding away, doing my little thing, you know...another 150 photographs hot off the press. Now they're saying I'm at a "funny age." What the hell does that mean? There's nothing funny about being 28. They tell me I'm going to be really hot when I get into my thirties. I say, "O.K.--fine. I'm a patient guy." More bars, more baths. Nobody's

3

telling me to wait until my face fills in <u>there</u>. Who gives a fuck about a face when all that matters is two hands and a crotch? I survived worse things than impatience anyway. I was my father's son and I survived. I served in Nam and I survived. I came out and I survived.

A QUIET END
by Robin Swados

Max - 30s - New York City - Present
Max is the intellectual of the trio; an ex-teacher who struggles with grim resolve to accept the decisions he has made in life. When Jason, his lover, arrives to bring him back to their apartment, Max reveals his anger and frustration with his illness.

MAX: You're asking me to open up my heart all over again. I closed it a long time ago. Even before I stopped seeing you. There's been great comfort--great safety in my isolation. *(Pause.)* I'm very used to my life now. Everything's come tumbling down on my head in the past few months, like an avalanche. A huge, incredible noise, and then silence. Silence and sickness. At night, steam blasts out of the radiator and I shiver in a cold sweat. During the day I feel like I'm burning up even as the ice forms on the inside of the window. I lie here staring up at the ceiling, soaking the sheets in the sweat of my past mistakes, choking back the bile which seems continually to rise in my throat. Is it anger that makes it rise, or just another nameless malady? Is it even my bile--my sweat--or someone else's mixed with mine, someone whose arms and legs I tangled with some night years ago? And him--the other guy--the one who casually chatted me up in some noisy, smoke-filled room somewhere--or maybe he didn't even bother to chat me up. Maybe he just felt me up instead. What about him? You think he's lying somewhere too, desperately wondering, and knowing he'll never know, who was responsible for his imminent demise? Which one is it? Which one?

A SILENT THUNDER
by Eduardo Ivan Lopez

Santana - 20s - Okinawa - 1960s
Santana is a US Marine preparing to leave his present station on
Okinawa. A turn of events have placed him in a hotel room
with Kimiyo, a beautiful young woman who is the daughter of
his tailor. Santana is a Viet Nam vet haunted by past tragedy,
but feels comfortable with Kimiyo. Here, he describes what it
was like growing up in an orphanage as a Puerto Rican.

SANTANA: But one thing you do learn in the States is that you
gotta be from somewhere. 'Cause the minute you walk on the
streets, somebody is gonna ask you what you are. And if you say
you're an American, they're gonna come back with "Yeah, I know
that, but what are you? Where are you from? Where do your
parents come from?" It's not enough that you're an American. You
gotta be from someplace else. And when you come from an
orphanage, you're from nowhere. *(Pause.)* I remember when I was
a kid in the orphanage. We would divy up into groups. The black
kids would go around braiding their hair and calling themselves
Africans. And we'd go around jiving and walking with our backs
hunched, slapping each other in the hands 'cause that was the way
Puerto Ricans acted on the streets and in the movies. What did we
know? We just copied everything people said was Puerto Rican.
Until one day--when I was eighteen--I went to Puerto Rico and found
out that I wasn't Puerto Rican at all. When I went into my Puerto
Rican act there,...they laughed at me. They couldn't even
understand my Spanish. They just laughed. Laughed at me as if I
were a clown.
[KIMIYO: Not worry, Santana-san.]
SANTANA: That's when I realized I didn't belong. So I stopped
being a Puerto Rican and joined the Marine Corps. They gave me
a uniform, and nobody cared what I was. 'Cause I was a marine--
and that's something. And that's what I am...So you see, I have no
need of those words anymore.

6

A SILENT THUNDER
by Eduardo Ivan Lopez

Santana - 20s - Okinawa - 1960s
After awaking from a terrible nightmare, Santana finally reveals that he feels responsible for the death of Keller, his friend and fellow Marine. He describes they're being sent to Viet Nam and the grisly events that led to his friend's death.

SANTANA: You won't tell nobody?...That was stupid. Who you gonna tell...First, you gotta understand that I'm a good Marine, as good as anybody. I went through boot camp, seen some action and I've done the job when I had to. I've even been decorated a few times. So I ain't no slouch, you know? It's important you know that 'cause I don't want you to think I don't pack the gear. I'm as tough as any of them. But you know,...*(He thinks back for a moment.)* when they first sent me over to Viet Nam, I was just a boot. Fresh out of basic training. I didn't know anything. I had less than a year in...Anyway, we are out in the field and the company commander says he's got reports that there was enemy activity a few miles north of our camp. The lieutenant asked for volunteers to check out the area, to see if the reports were true. So me and two other guys volunteered. What did we know? We figured it'd be easy duty. Anything was better than digging trenches for latrines. Anyhow, the three of us and a sergeant set out to reconnoiter the situation. When we got about a half mile from the camp,...all hell broke loose. *(He pauses.)* There were bullets flying from everywhere. The sergeant got it first, right in the side of the face. Then Milks got it. Well, I just started running. I ran right into the bush. This other guy, Keller, was right behind me. We didn't know where to go, so we stayed put, hoping they wouldn't come after us. We were scared shit the two of us. *(He looks at her questioningly.)* I mean, it wasn't supposed to be that way. They weren't supposed to be there. They were supposed to be miles up north. But there they were, all over the place. I figured that was it. It was all over. I had never seen anybody get killed before. And all

7

of a sudden, two of my friends are dead, and we're next. Keller knew it too. He kept looking at me with big eyes, wondering what we were gonna do to stop it. The sun was going down, so we dug in. We dug and dug into that ground until we couldn't dig no more. I kept hoping our guys had heard the shots and that they come to help us. But nobody came. It was just the two of us in that jungle...in the dark. We couldn't even see our hand in front of our face it was so black...*(Beat.)* And then they started. "Hey, America, give up. You gonna die." That kinda stuff. I never prayed before, but I was praying that night. I remembered what they use to tell us at boot camp. How we had to be tough. How no marine ever gave up...Well, I never figured it was gonna be like that. Alone and scared in the middle of nowhere with the mosquitoes eating your eyes out. I didn't wanna die, not there, not then. It wasn't fair. I hadn't lived yet. I was nineteen years old. I hadn't done anything or seen anything. Nobody knew who I was. And if I died, nobody would know I ever existed. *(He lets out a rueful laugh.)* There wouldn't even be a place to send the body. I thought of giving up. But then I remembered what they taught us at I.T.R. Recon patrols don't take prisoners. And they weren't about to take any. So I just lay there in the hole I had dug and died. Everytime I'd hear a branch crack or a bush rustle, I'd die. I died a thousand times that night. Then Keller started calling out to me. At first, he just wanted to make sure I hadn't run out on him. I told him to keep quiet, but he was scared too, I guess. Every once in a while he'd call. And then the V.C. picked up on it and started calling me by name. "Hey, Santana, why you wanna die?"...They kept it going all night. At least until I dozed off...Then I heard it. The crawling. Bodies scraping against the ground. I knew they were coming for us even before I heard them. They were close, real close. I grabbed my rifle and aimed it at the noise and fired. I couldn't see them, but I could hear their screams as the bullets would find them. I fired at the flash of their rifles. I fired at everything until I had nothing left...Then I leaned back against the wall of the hole and waited for them. *(He wipes away the tears.)* I waited until I saw the first light come through the trees. Then I heard the footsteps, a lot of them. This figure stepped at the edge of my hole, and I closed my eyes and waited for it to come. "Hey, Santana. Are you all right?" I opened my eyes, and there was Corporal Bridges looking down at me. He helped me out of the foxhole, and then I saw what I had done. *(He begins to sob.)* It was Keller. He was right next to my hole dead. Bullet holes all over him. I didn't know he was out there. I never heard him. He was just lying there with his head chopped off.

AT THE STILL POINT
by Jordan Roberts

Rod - 40s - A Home on the Hudson River, NY - Present
Billy has traveled from Utah to the Hudson River with the ashes
of his friend, Joey, who has died of AIDS. Billy searches for
Rod, Joey's older brother at a party at his house on the river but
cannot bring himself to tell Rob of Joey's death. Here, the
affable Rod tells Billy a story of the first time that he ever went
swimming in the river.

ROD: I refused to go in it. For years when I was a boy. The
family would all be swimming, it was a hundred degrees. It didn't
matter. I wasn't going in. And one day, I was five, four or five,
and there was this big, fat lady out there. Just this...huge woman.
And she was laughing. Laughing louder than you can imagine. Just
roaring. And I thought, now what the heck is that woman laughing
at? She's in this...Monster! This horrible monster. She should be
screaming. What is she doing?
[BILLY: Talking. Probably.]
[ROD: No. She was alone.]
[BILLY: Talking to the river.]
ROD: [Huh. Maybe.] My father picked me up. Right over there.
And just started to walk toward the laughing lady. I was screaming
my little head off. But he's got me, facing me, holding me out in
front of him. And I'm looking down, watching him disappear into
the Monster. Shins, knees, thighs, bathing trunks...and then I feel
it on my toes, and I know I'm going in it, and I freeze. Dead still,
silent. "I surrender." *(laughs)* You remember the first time? You
just throw in the towel to it. Of course the fat lady was laughing!
This was no Monster at all. It was nothing like...anything. Oh!
There I go again. My friends know how to shut me up. Strangers
just have to keep still. I hadn't thought about her in years.

AUGUST SNOW
by Reynolds Price

Neal Avery - 20s - North Carolina - 1937
Neal Avery is a young man who is being pulled in many
different directions at once. His wife resents the time he spends
with Porter, his best friend from childhood. His mother resents
the fact that he's gotten married. Porter wishes that he and Neal
could run away and be adventurers. Here, Neal reveals that no
one who loves him really knows him.

NEAL: One thing I know I'm not is conceited. So believe what I
say, in this one respect. The trouble, my whole life, has been this--
people fall for me, what they *think* is me. They mostly call it love,
and it generally seems to give them fits. They think life can't go on
without me--when I know life can go on in the dark if they blind
you, butcher you down to a torso, stake you flat on a rank wet floor
and leave you lonesome as the last good soul.

Neal Avery can't save the *shrubbery* from pain, much less
human beings. It may be the reason I act so bad to Taw and my
mother and Porter, my friend. It may be why I'm soaked to the ears
so much of the time---*I know I'm me,* an average white boy with all
his teeth, not Woodrow Wilson or Baby Jesus or Dr. Pasteur curing
rabies with shots.

Who on God's round Earth do they think I am? Who would
patch their hearts up and ease their pain? If I stand still here for
many years more, won't they wear me away like the Sphinx or a
doorsill, just with the looks from their famished eyes?

If I wasn't a Methodist, if this wasn't home, wouldn't I be
well advised to strip and run for the nearest desert cave and live
among wolves or crows or doves? Wouldn't they simply elect me
gamekeeper?

Am I ruined past help? Could I take ten steps on my own--
here to there--much less flee for life, for my good and theirs?

AUGUST SNOW
by Reynolds Price

Porter Farwell - 20s - North Carolina - 1937

Porter Farwell is a clerk in Avery's clothing store where he expects to work for the rest of his life. He has always lived in this small southern town and has grown to crave the anonymity it affords. Here Porter comments on the danger of revealing too much of your true nature to people who know you well.

PORTER: In a town this size, everybody's known your family since the Seven Years' War; so you have to live most of your life in code--little signals and fables for the kind and wise, not actual touch or plain true words. That's been all right by me most times; it keeps you from having to make up your mind too fast, or ever.

For years you can walk around some strong magnet and never ask why or be told to explain. Then when you least expect it, somebody you've known from the dark of the womb will step up and reach for the trunk of your life and shake it like a cyclone, and you'll shed your apples in full public view.

It happened to me my first year in high school, fourteen years old--English class, of course. Miss Speed Brickhouse went round the room asking everybody what they hoped to be; and everybody answered some sensible way--storekeeper, bank teller, practical nurse. Then she called on me--"Porter, what's your plan?"

I was already helping at Avery's store--Neal and I on Saturdays--and I figured I'd sell men's clothing for life. But what I said was what slipped out. To Miss Speed's withered face, and twenty-six children vicious as bats, I said, "I hope to be a lighthouse for others."

Miss Speed tried to save the day by saying the church was the noblest career, but everybody knew she was wrong, and they *howled*--right on through Commencement three whole years later.

I found the strength to hold my ground though, and I never explained. I knew I'd found, and told, the truth--a real light, for safety, in cold high seas.

Not for *others* though; I lied in that--just for Neal Avery, the one I'd long since chosen as being in special need and worthy of care. I may well have failed.

12

BRILLIANT TRACES
by Cindy Lou Johnson

Henry Harry - 20s - Alaska - Present
Rosannah is a confused young woman who leaves her fiance at the altar, jumps into her car and then drives as far as she can before a blizzard forces her to seek refuge in the converted barn occupied by Henry Harry, a young man who has been devastated by life. The two slowly reveal insights into their inner torments as the storm continues to rage outside. Henry Harry has accidently burned Rosannah's satin wedding slippers in an attempt to dry them. Frustrated by his feelings of inadequacy, he tells her of his young daughter, Annabelle, and how he let her down as well.

HENRY HARRY: You came in here, in the middle of the night, freezing to death, wearing paper shoes...little, tiny, paper... *(Turning on her fiercely.)* you don't know what life is like for me. You don't begin to know. I have tried always to steer clear of whatever this stuff is--all this--stuff, but I cannot. It finds me. It eats me up. It eats me up and never fully destroys me. No. It leaves shreds of me, just shreds--to come back for later. I was a kid--you know--just hanging out--and I met this girl, Nora, and she got knocked up--I mean by me. I'm not trying to remove myself, even if I felt removed at the time. Even if I felt like I was living in the freezer. So I went to live with her, take care of her. I never really loved her, but she got sick and needed help and since I had got her in this mess--I don't know--I just went. And then she had this little baby. We called her Annabelle. And it was like--I just woke up forever. I loved her. From just the minute she was born. That's what love is--something that just overcomes you and you can't stop it. So I stayed. And when Annabelle got to be about three, she had all these dolls she played with. And these dolls had little tiny clothing and even little rings and bracelets--so sometimes you might look on the floor and find some tiny little silver thing--looks like it's made out of tinfoil, but you *never, never* threw those things away

13

because they belonged to Annabelle--I mean to one of her little dolls. And for her, these things were *precious*. Even their little shoes were precious. I was constantly finding these little doll shoes all over the house and saving them for her, and she would be so happy to see that long lost shoe and put it on her little doll's foot. What I'm saying is--I could make her happy that way, just by finding a tiny little shoe...so some nights, after she was asleep, I would get down on my hands and knees and just scour the living room floor where she played, just in hopes that I would find a little shoe or something--and the next day make her happy--but then, one time, I was sweeping up and not really paying attention, and I think out of the corner of my eye, I saw this little blue thing go into the dustpan--you know--but my mind was preoccupied and *anyway,* you can't just be alert every single minute, so I just threw it in the trash, and the very next morning, the *very next,* she comes downstairs with this barefoot doll, looking for a little blue shoe--she's lost one of her shoes, and I *knew* immediately, but I mean you can't just go through the garbage every time a little tiny blue shoe gets lost, so I lied--I mean it wasn't really lying because I didn't know for sure that that was the thing I'd thrown away, but it was lying because I did know--and *now*--all the time I think about that lie--all the time. And some days I imagine myself going through the garbage and finding that shoe and washing it and giving it to her and she's so very happy, so very happy--so when you left those shoes out--what could I do? You see my situation? They were not *nothing*. They were not nothing lying there. They were *something*. I had to do something with them. I had no choice. I just put them under the broiler and put it on high heat. Here! *(He runs to the broiler and takes out the broiler pan, with the burnt shoes. He brings it over to Rosannah.)* There!

CANTORIAL
by Ira Levin

Warren Ives - 20s-30s - New York City - Present
Warren and Lesley have moved into a new home that happens
to be a converted synagogue. They are very happy until they
hear the singing. It seems that their new home is also inhabited
by the ghost of the synagogue's cantor. Warren, a non-Jew,
angrily confronts the musical spirit and tells him to leave.

WARREN: THIS IS *OUR* HOME! IT BELONGS TO *US* NOW!
It's not gonna be a synagogue ever again! TV in the Ark, not a
Torah! And that's the way it's gonna stay! *(Inspiration strikes.) If*
you're lucky...! *IF you're lucky!* You hear me, Kahzin? If you
sing one more note *we're gonna sell!* WE CAN'T LIVE HERE
WITH YOU! *(He waits. Silence.)* If we have to sell,
Mister...*(Raises his right hand.)*...as God as my witness...*we're
selling to MOSLEMS!* I kid you not! There's every ethnic group
you can dream of in this city and there are Moslems here too, you
can bet your *tookus!*
[LESLEY: There's a community in Brooklyn!]
WARREN: You hear that? A community in Brooklyn!
Overcrowded! *Dying to move into Manhattan if only they can find
someplace to pray!* And oh, are we ever gonna make them a
tempting offer!...*You hear me? (He races up the spiral stairs, and
leaning at the roof from the topmost curve sings cantorially.)*
M a a a a a a a a a a z z z z z z z l e m m m m m m m m m m s !
Maaaaaaaaaaaaaaaazzzleh-eh-eh-eh-eh-eh-eh-ehemmmmmmms!
(Finds his breath, pulls himself together.) Just one more note. As
God is my witness.

DIVIDENDS
by Gary Richards

Bernie - 60s-70s - New York - Present
Bernie is an elderly Jew who is dying. He and his wife have
returned to New York from Florida in order to be with their
family at the end. Bernie's grandson, Neal, is an artist living in
the Village. When he confronts Bernie with his own fears of
death, Bernie offers his own vision of how life should be
ordered.

BERNIE: You know, Neal, sometimes I think that God got it all
backwards. You should die first. Right? Get it over with. That
makes sense, yes? Then they take you out of the ground, dust you
off, so you can go into retirement. And for twenty-five years you
play some golf, you play some canasta down in Florida with your
friends. And when you get too young, they take away all your
benefits, so you have to go to work for forty years. Then you have
to stop working so you can go to college. Where you study a little,
you drink a little, you chase girls a little. You graduate, and then
it's on to high school. Where you study a little, you drink a little,
you chase girls a little. Everything gets simpler. You have less and
less to worry about, so you don't know from far-tshadikt. Then you
become a little boy and all you do is play. Pretty soon you're a
baby. You eat, sleep, and poop. Finally, you spend nine months
floating in oblivion. It's warm. It's cozy. And eventually you
become just a twinkle in someone's eye. (I think that when I get up
there I'll suggest it to him.) *(pause)* But it doesn't happen this way.
Sometimes it doesn't happen like you thought it would.

DIVIDENDS

by Gary Richards

Bernie - 60s-70s - New York - Present

Bernie was never bar mitzvahed, and now that the end is near, he feels that it's important to have the ceremony. His great inner strength and determination carry him through the proceedings and he uses this very special occasion to express his deep love for his family and the life that they have shared.

BERNIE: The rabbi told me that in biblical times, it was said that one should live to be three score and ten. That's seventy years old. And anything more than that, you should feel lucky. I'm eighty-three. I've had thirteen years more. Thirteen! <u>Now</u> is the time I should have a bar mitzvah. If I had a bar mitzvah back then, it would not have meant as much. Maybe bar mitzvahs are wasted on the young. I stand here before you on my special day. A day I've longed for all my life. And I guess I just want to say thank you. I'd like to thank my children, my grandchildren, and my great grandchildren for the love and support you have shown to me today. I would like to thank my grandson, Neal. Thank you Neal for helping make one of my dreams come true. And I would like to thank my wife. Bessie. She insisted that I go out and buy a brand new suit even though she knows I'll wear it only twice. Thank you, Bessie. For fifty-nine and a half years I got up every morning and went out to get you a fresh bagel with Farmer's cheese and the Daily News. I always considered it a great honor. You will not miss the bagel as much as I will miss getting it for you.

To think all of this has come from love of an ordinary man and woman. Maybe the ordinariness of my life is what made it so special.

Today! Today is my future! And my future is paying me back! My investment is giving me such a return like I never dreamed! A return of love. A return of life.

You know, you live your life, it takes all your time, and then you die. That time is all we have. That time is what we call our life! That time is our journey.

I...I maybe did some good...provided...on my journey, in my time. *(pause)* I love you all. "Today I am a man."

17

EACH DAY DIES WITH SLEEP
by José Rivera

Augie - 50s-60s - New York - Present
Augie is the boorish and brutish patriarch of a clan boasting 21 children. He is a man filled with hatred and uncontrollable lusts. Here, he describes a typical day in rather graphic detail.

AUGIE: Aww, my day <u>sucked</u>. It started this morning with Ping screaming because Sylvia was wailing on his face with a crescent wrench. Then it's Antonio screaming 'cause he's drowning in the blood of Ping's massive nose bleed and would have died if I hadn't performed mouth-to-mouth CPR on him. Then, after breakfast, Rosaline sets Anita's cat on fire and the cat's screaming, running around with its bubbling organs and it's sizzling eyes, and then Primitivo's brought home by the cops in handcuffs for extorting money in school from the first graders, and Marcus Junior's got an olive pit so far up his nose it's playing pinball with his goddamn brains, and this social worker tells me the way out of my poverty is sterilization. "I WILL NOT BE STERILIZED," I said, as I threw her through a window on the third floor.

EACH DAY DIES WITH SLEEP
by José Rivera

Augie - 50s-60s - New York - Present
Nelly is the only one of Augie's children who cares enough to
see that he gets safely into bed every night. Despite her father's
efforts to keep her in thrall, she has fallen in love with the
handsome Johnny, who returns her love. Paralyzed from the
waist down in an accident, Augie despairs when Nelly and
Johnny marry and move to California. The helpless Augie rages
at being left alone with his wife, who has taken a lover.

AUGIE: CUT IT OUT! I'm not going to sit here and quietly
decompose while you and your boyfriend sin against God and nature.
(Augie bangs on the door with the crutch.) A WOMAN YOUR
AGE! MOTHER OF TWENTY-ONE CHILDREN! HAVE SOME
RESPECT FOR THE SACRED VOWS WE TOOK. WILL YA?!
(He pounds on the door and the laughter subsides.) THINK
YOU'RE TWENTY-ONE YEARS OLD AGAIN? Huh? Think you
still have something to give a man? Huhh? What do you have? A
COUPLE OF MOLDY ORGASMS? *(He bangs on the wall.)* AND
WHY DON'T I HEAR MY CHILDREN WALKING AROUND?
Where are my babies? I wasn't so bad to them! All I hear are the
groans of the bears and the screams of the wild monkeys. HAS
ANYBODY FED THOSE ANIMALS? They can smell me. They
know I'm defenseless. OKAY--TELL MY CHILDREN I'LL
REINSTATE BIRTHDAYS. HAPPY BIRTHDAY TO ALL THEM
SNOTNOSES! *(He bangs on wall.)* And someone has to come here
and kill the mold growing on my arms! *(A spotlight on Nelly asleep
on the couch.)* And I want to know where what's-her-name is. My
daughter. The only child in this zoo that treated my with due
respect. She was here once. She opened windows for me. And
sweet air swept into the room with busy fingers that cleaned the filth
from my skin...and hot sunlight cooked every last cold corner of this
room and blasted the night to pieces...it was great! I saw little
pieces of night, shrieking and squeaking and scrambling under all the

19

furniture and hiding in all the cracks of the floor, because of her. *(Augie dials the phone. It rings in Nelly's house. She wakes up. She looks at the phone. Augie waits, then slams down the phone.)* I can BRING her back. All I have to do is remember her name. I know all their names. I can name all my kids. Oscar, Maritza, Nilda, Heriberto, Carlos, Marcos, Beto, Lizbeth, Jesus, Felicia, Che, Gloria, Antonio, Anita, Rosaline, Primitivo, Ping, Sylvia, Linda, and Freddie. *(Counts on his fingers.)* THAT'S TWENTY. Oscar, Maritza, Nilda, Heriberto, Carlos, Marcos, Beto, Lizbeth, Jesus, Felicia, Che, Gloria, Antonio, Anita, Rosaline, Primitivo, Ping, Sylvia, Linda, Freddie and, and, and...who? Goddammit, tell me. WHO IS SHE?! I CAN STILL SMELL HER IN THIS ROOM.

ELLIOT LOVES
by Jules Feiffer

Phil - 30s-40s - New York City - Present
Elliot and Joanna have fallen in love and Elliot wishes to
introduce her to his friends. When they have all gathered, Phil,
a close friend of Elliot's who has recently quit drinking,
comments on the possibility that the world's greatest innovations
were most likely thought of while their inventors were in a state
of intoxication.

PHIL: Everyone talks about support groups for alcoholics. You
know? Somebody should talk about countersupport groups. "Come
on, one little drink won't hurt you." I've never been offered so
many drinks in my life since I went on the wagon. The shit you get
away with drunk. You know? You can't drop water bags off a
terrace sober.
[ELLIOT: You never did that.]
PHIL: Not here. A couple of years ago. Condoms filled with
water. I can't remember the name of the girl I woke up in bed with
that night. You know? But I remember the condoms filled with
water. That's what I have nostalgia for. The freedom. I'm a
tightass sober; I'm a free man drunk. You know? I talked women
into bed I wouldn't have the nerve to open my mouth to sober. I
made friends. You know? I could never talk up to people the way
Larry does. You know? But five or six bourbons, I could tell
jokes. I don't know how to tell a joke, but I could tell 'em drunk.
You know? I was better at everything drunk...except marriage and
work. You know? And I prefer drinking to both. I bet JFK could
put it away. Bet he could hold his liquor too. I bet he was a couple
of sheets to the wind all through the Cuban missile crisis. I know
I'd be. Adlai Stevenson and the Joint Chiefs in one room, Judith
Exner in the next. You know? Can you imagine me peeing off a
balcony with JFK? Teddy maybe, not Jack. Jack was a classy
drunk. I'm more like Teddy. Black guys--they really pull out the
jams drunk. Hispanics too. They get crazy--you know?--the music

and everything. Crazy. They get high on the noise. Not Jews, though. When Jews get drunk they confuse it with their role in the universe. They don't have fun, they have insights. You can just bet that Einstein had a bag on the night he came up with $E=MC^2$. *(Elliot laughs.)* You think that's funny? You want to put money on Freud being smashed the night he came up with the Oedipus complex? *(Elliot turns away, smiling.)* Karl Marx--he came up with communism tanked. You know, Elliot? Four in the morning, bombed out of his mind. If he hadn't made notes, he would have forgotten it the next morning and we're all better off. Right? Right. You know? Wasps drunk--Wasps drunk are no different from Wasps sober. You know? Upper-class Wasps, I mean, upper-class. Lower-class--they know how to have a good time. But upper-class Wasps, you know--you know?--they get paranoid drinking that, that they'll lose control. Right? Right. An ex-altar boy like me, you know, I only feel in control when I'm drunk; but Wasps, who really are in control, when they get drunk they get afraid that they'll lose it. You're not smiling. That's okay too. This is the best time I've had since I quit drinking, and it's because you don't care if I'm alive or dead. If you're just holding that glass, Elliot, and not drinking on account of me, you don't have to. I'm past that.

ELLIOT LOVES
by Jules Feiffer

Bobby - 30s-40s - New York City - Present
Elliot, Joanna, Phil, Larry and Bobby have all gathered in
Bobby's study for an evening of drink and story telling. The
conversation drifts to contemporary theater, and Bobby is
reminded of a scene in "Fences" that was reminiscent of an
event in his childhood.

BOBBY: My father died at forty-two, which is my next birthday.
From the time I was fourteen, I was bigger and stronger and better
coordinated than my father. Not as heavy, though. No way. My
father was the original butterball. Mr. Five-by-Five. Loved to
throw that ball. Did he ever! And moved pretty good for a man his
girth. He had these dainty little feet, goddamnedest feet! My
mother's feet were bigger. Toes the size of cucumbers. An ox, my
mother. But my father, you understand, he had a good arm on him.
And he could rifle a throw in from right field, nail a man turning
third, never make it home. I saw him do it more than once. But he
couldn't get around on a fastball. This particular Sunday--did I say
I'm fourteen?--I struck him out twice. Fathers-and-sons game.
Hyde Park, you understand, and I was a big kid. Oh, was I! On
my mother's side they're all six feet and over. But I worshipped the
man. Like in *Fences*. Father and son. Like in *Bambi*. Where the
stags fight. So now I struck out Bambi's father, and he has trouble
meeting my eye. I'm fourteen years old and I don't weigh a
hundred and thirty, and two strikeouts later I'm king of the stags.
My father abdicates. Everybody struck the old fool out! It was
never the same.

THE FILM SOCIETY
by Jon Robin Baitz

Jonathan Balton - 40s - South Africa - 1970
The tragedy of South Africa's system of Apartheid is reflected
in the relationships among the white faculty of the Blenheim
School for Boys in Natal Province. Jonathan Balton is a man
torn between his hatred for the system and his need to survive
within it. Recently promoted to headmaster at Blenheim, Balton
is faced with the unpleasant task of firing Nan, his longtime
friend. Before doing so, he tells a story of his childhood in
which he was unable to slaughter a cow.

BALTON: No. Just tired out. I was thinking of the farm. Every
Saturday night, father'd give one of the cows to the natives. A treat.
Few farms did that. But actually, it was no sacrifice, just a small
feeble animal. And yet, canecutters, herd boys, all of them...would
look forward to Saturday night. The compound would come alive.
That mad Zulu pop music on the Bantu radio. I'd sit in nanny's lap,
watching. It was all very festive. *(beat)* I was mostly interested in
the killing of the cow. Used to be, they used a knife, and that was
vivid, very much a thing of the bush. To see the creature's dull eyes
flashing, hooves scraping at the dirt as the knife was led across the
throat--and the blood running into a gourd on the ground. But the
part that fascinated me the most, was when it was dead. Its
evisceration. The skin drawn slowly back, and the veins exposed,
black blood clotting into the reddish dust of the compound, which
would be dead quiet, sombre. Little ivory coloured and purple-hued
sacks filled with bile and acid and urine. Balloons of undigested
grass, bones cracked, and muscles pulsing gently, as a fire was
readied, and the tongue, the great curled muscle, unravelled, cut out,
and the teeth and jaw laid bare. *(pause)* But it is one Saturday in
particular that I remember. It was my birthday, and I was given the
honour of killing the cow. I was eleven. The knife was dispensed
with, and my father gave me a pistol with tiny silver-tipped bullets.
I was to blow out the brains from a little spot between the eyes, and

this death had none of the ritual of the knife. It was an assassination and I believe the natives knew this. Unbearable to have this cow led to me, docile, and uncomplaining. She was tied to a post, with a little strand of rope, and I tried to do the thing very quickly. But you see, I did not do a proper job of it. And the bullet ricochetted of her skull and down into the jaw--this shattered pulp of bone and blood, through which she screamed, you see, as I recall it. And tore loose from her feebly tied rope. And there she was, with saliva, and plasma all about, bolting into the cane fields, everyone stunned. She was gone. And I stood there. Frozen. *(pause)* And I looked up, and saw my father standing on the verandah of the main house with my mother--and he said something to her, and went inside, and nanny came to me. And of course, by this time, I was crying. The natives staring at their feet--mortified. No laughter--which might have been preferable. *(pause)* And then my father came out of the house with his shotgun, got on his horse, and rode into the field, and there was a single muffled blast, and nanny put me to bed. A quiet supper that night, no singing or dancing, and of course, not long after, we moved into the city--my mother's idea. So I was just thinking about my father, and all.

FLORIDA GIRLS
by Nancy Hasty

Reverend Thompson - 30s-50s - Florida - Present
Grandmother drags the family to her fundamentalist church, where they are subjected to this hellfire and brimstone sermon delivered by the Reverend Thompson, who is more showman than a man of the cloth. Today his topic of obsession is the cosmetics industry and how it makes "jezebels" out of young women.

REVEREND THOMPSON: Looking out I am pleased to see so many young people in the congregation...because TONIGHT begins the YOUTH segment of our revival! And tonight's message is entitled "Daughters of Light--or--Daughters of Darkness." You know, I've only been in Crestview since yesterday, but it seems everywhere I look I see signs for a beauty contest Saturday night. A BEAUTY CONTEST! *(He crosses to the pulpit and opens the Bible:)* Let us turn now in our Bibles to Second Kings where we find these words...*(He reads:)* "Jezebel did paint her face, so they threw her down, and her blood was splattered on the wall and they trod her underfoot. And when they went to bury her, they found no more of her than the...skull...and the feet and the palms of her hands. THE DOGS DID EAT THE FLESH OF JEZEBEL, and THIS...is the work of the Lord!" *(He crosses down front.)* Now, I know what you are thinking. You are thinking yourselves..."Why--does Reverend Thompson speak to US of Jezebels?" Looking out, I see only good, Godly young Christian women. I see faces that plain and unadorned, shine with Gawd's beauty. *(He finds Nancy in the crowd.)* Little one, what is your name again? Nancy! Stand Nancy! *(Once again, he eyes her outfit.)* Now, tell all these people how old you are. Louder! They can't hear you in the back! *(Shouting for her:)* Twelve years old! Surely that young face shines with Gawd's beauty! *(He motions her back into her pew.)* Is there anything more precious than a young girl's pure and Godly face? *(Pointing to various churchmembers in rapid succession:)* But!

FLORIDA GIRLS

There is! A Devil! And his name is! SATAN! And he HATES...a Godly face. He takes on many shapes and many guises. He is everywhere at every time. This Satan never sleeps. Now let me show you how this Satan works!! *(The next speech is mimed out to the smallest detail. It is a fine performance.)* Mother is ironing in the kitchen. She has the radio tuned to a gospel station. But then, some household chore calls her to another room, and her young daughter happens by--and turns the dial! SUDDENLY--instead of God's word, we have Satan spitting out LUST! And before she knows it, her body begins to GYRATE to Satan's rhythm. But is Satan satisfied with just a dance? No...no! Now she must dress for him and paint her face for him and soon she is sneaking off to the high school to be in a beauty contest--SPONSORED BY THE BOARD OF EDUCATION! And then she's coming home in back of some boy's car and then...not coming home at all! And it all began because a radio dial was left unattended. SATAN WANTS YOUR DAUGHTERS! He's waiting for them in a radio. He's waiting for them in a tube of lipstick. He's waiting for them down on Main Street to lure them into the beauty shops! He wants to pour them into seductive clothing and annointst their bodies with oils and myrrhr and Chanel No. 5! SATAN WANTS YOUR DAUGHTERS! He wants them in a beauty contest! What do they do in a beauty contest? I FOUND OUT! They parade themselves--almost naked-- before all the men of Crestview! Look, look, look. Touch, touch, touch. Strut, strut, strut! How many of you sitting here today know some young girl in Crestview--who wants to be in a beauty contest, who is going to roast in hell? How many of you sitting here today know that you yourself are in danger of temptation? Are you just going to sit there and let it happen? Or--are you going to stand up-- in front of this congregation--in front of God himself--and say: NO! I WILL NOT BE A JEZEBEL! Then get up off that pew and come down this aisle. Come down this aisle now and say-- *(He motions to the pianist:)*...hit it, Sister Miriam...*(The thundering chords of "Just As I Am" fill the church.)*...and say: YES! TO GOD!!!

GAL BABY
by Sandra Deer

Tommy - 40s-50s - A Small Georgia Town - Present
Gal Baby's husband, Tommy, is on the edge. He's having an
affair and the bank is threatening to foreclose on the plantation.
He finally snaps under the pressure and explains to Gal Baby
why everyone's talking is driving him crazy.

TOMMY: Gal, shut up.

[GAL BABY: I'm sorry. It's just I have these things I need to tell
you. And if I don't you won't know them, and some of them may
be important. I mean, your messages from Sandy, for example.
You want your messages from Sandy, don't you?]

TOMMY: No, I don't. I want some peace and quiet. I want
someone to just be quiet and listen to me. Will you do that, Gal?
Will you be quiet and listen to me?

[GAL BABY: What is it, darling?]

TOMMY: Will you?

[GAL BABY: Yes.]

TOMMY: Everybody just talks and talks. I went to get my teeth
cleaned this morning and the girl started in like a radio. I couldn't
turn her off. I couldn't even turn her down. My mouth is full of
her hands and she's going ninety miles a minute. She kept asking
me questions, and like a fool I'd try to answer. She'd say, "Did you
and your wife see "Les Miserables" in London or New York?" and
I'd say *(mumbles London)*, and she laughed and said why didn't I
just listen and let her do the talking. But she keeps on asking me
questions, with no intention of having them answered.

[GAL BABY: Tommy, dental hygienists are trained to be friendly
like that.]

TOMMY: Then Rudie picked me up in the Rolls to go to Mother's
for lunch. We sat down at the table with mother, and I
complimented Rudie on the way the festival's been run this year. I
said I thought he was doing a nice job, and he sort of bounces a
little, you know the way he does? With just his shoulders? Like he

can't wait to say something, and keeps bouncing like that, and I'm trying to pay him a compliment, and before I can get the words out completely, he's bouncing and saying "Talk it up. Talk it up." Like a parrot. And then Sarah brings out this mock turtle soup, and I said, "Sarah, this is delicious. This is a beautiful meal." And Sarah said, "Tell 'em 'bout it, honey, tell 'em 'bout it." And Mother, you know how she bobs and sways and smiles? Like a marionette? She's swaying and smiling and sort of singing. "Keep on talking. Keep on talking." So there's Rudie squawking like a parrot, "Talk it up. Talk it up." And Sarah grinning, "Tell 'em about it, Honey." And my mother presiding over the mock turtle soup swaying like a goddam marionette and singing "Keep on talking. Keep on talking." And right there in the middle of lunch at my mother's Chippendale table with sunlight streaming in through the window, I lost it. I said, "Keep on talking! Can anybody stop? Would it be possible for one minute for everyone to just shut the fuck up?"
[GAL BABY: You didn't.]
[TOMMY: I did.]
[GAL BABY: In front of your mother? What did she do?]
TOMMY: She kept on talking. She didn't even hear me. I think I stood up then. And Mother said, "Son, are you all right?" And I said, "No ma'am. I don't feel too good. I think I'd better go." And I left. I walked over to the bus depot to get a taxi. I sat in the front with the driver. A boy about seventeen. He had earphones on playing music straight into his ears. It never even hit the air. And beside him on the seat was the Cliff's Notes for Lord of the Flies. I started crying. Something about that yellow and black Cliff's Notes filled with those mean little boys. I was actually sobbing. The boy didn't hear me because of the earphones. I turned my head and looked out the window until we got back to town.

THE HOLY TERROR
Melon Revised
by Simon Gray

Melon - 40s - England - Present

Melon, an irrepressible publisher who seems to teeter on the edge of sanity, addresses the ladies of the Cheltenham Women's Institute with various anecdotes of his life. Here he announces his suspicion that many of the ladies present have secretly written romance novels as a means of getting more love in their lives.

MELON: Oh, if you knew these authors as I do, ladies, deceitful in their deceptions even. The stories I could tell you--and, come to think of it, I know you ladies, too, yes, I do, *(Coyly)* not as ladies, I mean, naturally not, but what about all those pages on pages you've got squirrelled away in your bottom's drawers--desk drawers, desk drawers, that is. *(Lets out a yelp of laughter)* Oh, I'll bet there's more than just one or two of you, more than five or six of you, possibly even more than ten or twenty of you ladies who have a whole novel, a romance possibly, about some rugged chaps whipping off your bodice--no, no, I mean chap, *one* rugged chap whipping off not *your* bodice, of course, but the bodice of some loving and free spirited lass, eh? *(Chuckles)* Come on, ladies, own up! Or what about that serious and moving study, autobiographical-- with a whole poetic chapter on the trauma of your first period and so forth, eh? So forth, so forth, so forth. *(Increasingly mechanically, puts his hand to his head)* Ladies--ladies, did something happen to the lights? There was a moment there when I lost your--your faces. Your kindly, comforting--but I see you now, there you all are, kind um--um *(Looks down at his cards)*--and comfort--'Don't boast.' But we've had that one. Why does it keep turning up? 'Say sorry.' 'Don't boast.' 'Say sorry' *(Lispingly)*-- why do I keep telling myself to humiliate myself? Do I want to win your love? Can that be it? That I came all the way down here to Chislehurst, no Chelmsford, no Cheltenham, no--anyway, here, wherever it is--to win the love of you ladies? Do you want my love?

THE HOLY TERROR

Why should I want yours? Love, love, love, that's all people talk about, think about, write about, but the fact is *(Drawing himself up)*--I have merely come all the way down here to Chippingham to tell you the truth about my life. And it's not a boast, for which I therefore do not have to apologize, to say that I was--am, am--a great publisher who never, ever missed an opportunity, not a single opportunity, however remote and improbable--not a single *whiff* of an opportunity did I ever once miss--

INFINITY'S HOUSE
by Ellen McLaughlin

Indian - 30s-50s - The American Desert - Any Time
Set against a desert backdrop, "Infinity's House" tells the story
of three different eras in American history while an impassive
Southwestern Indian offers occasional allegorical and poetic
narratives. Here, he tells a story of man's fruitless quest to
become master of the universe.

INDIAN: Before everything else there was one man, the man we
call the Man Alone. He was like the White man Adam, and he was
very smart and very stupid, all at once. When he woke up into
Creation he found himself very beautiful, as indeed he was, as
indeed we all are. But all of his gifts of perception only served to
make him more suspicious. He looked at his foot. He said, "You
are so astonishing, the way you take so much weight, even though
you are so small, but you are too far below me, I can't watch you
well enough, I must find a way to keep an eye on you." So he cut
off his foot in order to see it better and he walked no more. He
learned nothing from the blood and pain, only more suspicion. Next
he looked at his hands. He said, "How is it you can do all these
things so well, I have only to think of something and you are doing
it. But you are also devious, so many fingers and so much skill, I
can't trust you, you will betray me some day." So he cut off his
hands and was satisfied for a time. Then, of course, his eyes
became a problem. They seemed to be always open, seeing more
than he could think about all at once. He blinded himself, and for
a moment his mind was quiet. But still he felt he wasn't yet his own
master. What was it? Something was still in him that was beyond
his control. And then he knew. His heart. Beating and beating
without end, alive within him. There was nothing for him to do but
to find a way to stop his own heart. And that he did, by throwing
himself onto a sharp stone. Finally he had subdued all the things
inside himself that he was not master of, and at last he could be
content. So.

INFINITY'S HOUSE
by Ellen McLaughlin

Oppenheimer - 40s-50s - The American Desert - Any Time
Here we find Oppenheimer, the creator of the Atomic Bomb,
wandering in the desert. He is a man haunted by his relentless
need to control and to be near madness.

OPPENHEIMER: Once mad, one never feels entirely in control
again. And control is so important. And I was mad. I stood for
hours in the winter of my twentieth year, the American in the British
lab, I stood for hours before a blackboard. All I knew was that I
was supposed to be able to think, that I was a theoretician. I thought
that meant that ideas would come to me, attracted like moths to
light. So I would wait for them, chalk in hand, attentive, a voice in
my head, my own, saying, "The point is, the point is, the point
is..." And days would pass, the light would do its slow, incremental
dance across the board. My hand, lifted, would throb with pain.
My mind, dark, attracted no moths. Only silence and the still voice
of my own soul pleading its tiny invocation. Long days,
unspeakably long days of me waiting for me to speak. I'm still
waiting. I hear others, always more clearly than I hear myself. And
I know that I am not in control. I regained my sanity, what I ever
had, which was some kind of appearance of life, the look of a
normal man. I ate, I slept, I talked, I went on. I seemed. But
always the fear has been there. That cool, insolent board, clean and
waiting. The silence, the futility. And I'm alone once more.
Frightened. Because I have learned something. Once you set
something in motion, it wants to take its course. All this fracturing
of life, breaking energy from mass, examining the unexaminable--
these things are not done without consequence. Things want to keep
splitting. There is no end to it. The soul itself unravels--the self
watching the self watching the self, a sickening infinity of mirrors
until life is overwhelming, action impossible. And these fractions
never rest, but enter us, their creators, and continue their work
within, riffling through the molecular structure, unbraiding the

33

familiar processes of the cell, and chaos bleeds invisibly throughout us, eating us with terrible division.   I think of Marie Curie, blindness overtaking her, her hands burning from radiation poisoning, continuing to split the world in her lab. It is no longer marks on a blackboard, but life itself.   The point is...the point is...the point is the more we try to control the less we are in control.

THE LISBON TRAVIATA
by Terrence McNally

Mendy - 40s - New York City - Present
Mendy is middle-aged, gay and a devotee of the opera. He is passionate about Maria Callas, and here talks on the phone to a young man from Portugal who may have seen Callas perform Traviata.

MENDY: No, horses and camels are *Aida*. I wish you could remember the singers as well as you do the animals. *Traviata* begins at a party. Everyone is drinking champagne and being very gay. I'll ignore that! And then the tenor's father, the baritone, comes in and ruins everything, as fathers will. And then there's a gambling scene and in the last act she reads a letter, *Teneste la promessa*, and dies. You remember that much? Then you definitely remember *Traviata*. Now try to describe the soprano who was singing Violetta. Violetta is the heroine. You're making me feel like Milton Cross. Skip it. Just tell me about the soprano. Other than the fact that you didn't like her, what can you tell me about her? "Lousy" is a strong word, Paul. So is "stunk." I don't care about your opinion as a matter of fact! It's her name I'm after. I think you heard Maria Callas. That's a good question. I loved her so much. I still do. Everything about her. Anything. I'll take crumbs when it comes to Maria. Her time was so brief. That's why I was hoping maybe you could tell me something about her I didn't know. She's given me so much: pleasure, ecstasy, a certain solace, I suppose; memories that don't stop. This doesn't seem to be such a terrible existence with people like her to illuminate it. We'll never see her like again. How do you describe a miracle to someone who wasn't there? Do yourself a favor. Put on one of her records. *Puritani* or *Sonnambula* or *Norma*. If what you hear doesn't get to you, really speak to you, touch your heart, Paul, the truth of it, the intensity of the feeling...well, I can't imagine such a thing. I don't think we could be friends. I know we couldn't. There's a reason we called her La Divina but if you don't even remember who sang

Traviata that night, there's no point in going on with this even if you did hear Callas. For people like you, it might as well have been Zinka Milanov. Skip that one too. Listen, thank you for your trouble. Enjoy the movie. No, I don't care what your grandfather thought of her either. The two of you heard the greatest singer who ever lived and you don't even remember it. Yes, she's dead, thanks to people like you! Murderer! I hope you hate the movie. *(He hangs up.)* God, I loathe the Portuguese.

THE LISBON TRAVIATA
by Terrence McNally

Mike - 20s-30s - New York City - Present
Mike and Stephen have been lovers for a long time. Mike
confronts Stephen with the disintegration of their relationship
citing alienation as the root of their now irreconcilable
differences.

MIKE: I haven't been your lover since the first night I said to
myself, "Who is this person lying at my side, this stranger, who
hasn't heard or held me since the last time it pleased him?" That's
the night I should have grabbed you by the shoulders and screamed,
"I don't want this, Stephen. I don't need just another warm body
next to mine. I'm much too needy to settle for so little. Look at
me. Love me. Be with me." Now I've waited too long. You
weren't even sleeping. You were reading. Your friend was on your
cassette player on your side of the bed. Maria Callas. You had
your back to me. I had my arm around you. I was stroking one of
your tits. I asked you how you thought I should handle Sarah--she
was coming up to New York and wanted to see me. It was the first
time since the divorce and I was scared. I'd hurt her in a way I was
ashamed of. I really needed you and you just shrugged and said
"You'll do the right thing" and turned the page. I didn't stop
stroking your tit but you weren't the same person anymore. Neither
was I. I kept my arm around you only because I was suddenly so
scared. I was as alone as I must have made Sarah feel. I was
holding on for dear life.

MAIDS OF HONOR
by Joan Casademont

Roger - 30s - Marblehead, MA - Present
Izzy and Annie want to stop their sister, Monica, from marrying a man they know is a crook. Roger is Monica's true love and the man she has left to marry the crooked banker. Roger arrives at her family's home on the evening before the nuptials are to take place and presents Izzy with Monica's diary, which she had evidently left behind when she left him. Roger tells Izzy that he refused to read through the diary and describes the events that led to the end of their relationship.

ROGER: She moves out on me one day with no warning after I have asked her, I have pleaded with her to please not move out on me ever until we have agreed that that's it, we can't make it. I mean we even went to this couples doctor together, she knew how I felt about it. I had two mothers die on me, you know? I have my own problems with being left. So what does she do? She moves out on me because I didn't show up at her birthday party because she didn't think it was important enough for her to come to a public health benefit that it took me months to set up. Of course it wasn't important enough. Nothing I did was ever that important to her. Okay, so I shoulda gone to her party anyway. I wasn't big enough, I was pissed. She still didn't have to move out and refuse to speak to me. If she really never wanted to see me again, she wouldn't have left this diary. You don't leave a diary behind unless you're still trying to get through to somebody in a totally ass backwards way, right?

MARY AND LIZZIE
by Frank McGuinness

Priest - 40s - Any Place - Any Time

An Irish priest has converted from Catholicism to Protestantism and now considers himself neither. In an allegorical speech, he calls for the "children of Ireland" to turn their backs on their faiths and look at both with new eyes.

PRIEST: Praise be to Christ who is King of the waters, mighty and wonderful in earth and water. Lead me, Aquinas, who doth walk in love and knowledge. Hear me, great Luther, in faith's defence. Shelter me, Calvin, in fate and fortitude. A mighty tower let me construct, an alphabet of God, ye prophets of Revelations. Let me recite for my people a service of splendour that they shall eat the fruits of love, of good and evil. From my hand and my mouth shall speak such truths that they who witness shall feel their breath turn to fire. And from this divine service I shall exclude my mother.

Turn, turn, ye Catholic damned, fear, fear for the error of your ways, fear as I feared for my many errors. I gave this body to the whore of Babylon, robed in the regalia of Catholic priests. I wear these raiments as penance and punishment. I saw the light that is Satan's throne. Children of Ireland, have you seen Satan? Children of Ireland, have you seen my mother? Do not listen to her lies and scandals. I am no Catholic, no Protestant. I worship both faiths with new eyes.

Shall I spell out the faith of the future? Christ is amongst us with a new commandment. Hate one another as I have hated you. Jesus it was who tempted Satan, promised him the throne of Rome. Satan agreed on one condition. Amend the commandments of the Lord. In this island I preach new religion. Where there is God, take his name in vain. Remember thou keep the Sabbath savage. Kill the honour of father and mother. Steal neighbour's wife and neighbour's goods. Convert, convert and covet, covet. *(Enter Old Woman.)* Wash ye in waters of revelation, dance in the beauty of virgin's blood.

[OLD WOMAN: Jesus, Mary and St. Joseph.]

PRIEST: Fear not the dawn of holy salvation, embrace the night of your new soul.

MASTERGATE
by Larry Gelbart

Wylie Slaughter - 50s-60s - Washington, DC - Present
In this satirical look at the Watergate and Iran-Contra scandals, the absurd nature of our bureaucracy is brought to hilarious and sometimes painful light. At the play's climax, Wylie Slaughter, the recently deceased head of the CIA, appears before the House Select Committee via a prerecorded hologram and informs all assembled that he was behind the insidious "Mastergate." He continues to warn that before his death, he set many other similar plans into action.

SLAUGHTER: I am Wylie Grimm Slaughter. September 24th, 1904-April 3rd, 1989. Having anticipated this hearing, I took great pains to produce what you see before you--a holographic image that creates the illusion that I am present in this room, whereas, you all know that I've passed away for reasons you've read in newspaper accounts, accounts prepared under my specific misdirection. I will, or course, answer no questions here today. This is no time for me to learn new tricks. Swearing me in, were it even remotely possible, would serve as little purpose now as it ever did in the past. I am not here to plead ignorance or to pass the buck. I am here to take responsibility for it all; to *bask* in your blame! At this moment in time--*your* time--Operation Masterplan will have self-destructed to the gleeful satisfaction of the media, those self-annointed guardians of the nation's interest. Let me state this one last time that I have never been opposed to the belief that the press has the right to print or broadcast everything it knows. I simply maintain that they don't have to know *everything*. If putting the freedom of this nation ahead of freedom for the press is a crime, then I am guilty! If putting the US ahead of the UP is treason, then wake the firing squad! For me, any means whatsoever is permissible to stave off the mortal danger that was posed when the first Red Dawn darkened the sky shining down on Karl Marx, as he dipped his pen in human suffering to write his infamous "Mein Kamphital!" Marxistism is not, however,

40

our only foe. The biggest threat exists here at home from those who spout the Constitution and the Bill of Rights, as though they owned them, for the purpose of aiding and abetting the malcontents who are sworn to destroy those very instruments! Firemen fighting for the rights of arsonists! These misguided dupes, as cancerous as any Communist cell, have permanated every level of society! *(Moving forward.)* But, rest assured, this country will be saved in spite of its principles! Mastergate was not the last operation I set in motion. Not by a long shot. Keep reading your morning headlines. Watch your nightly news. It's only a matter of time before you're "scandalized" by the stars of the next, inevitable Whatever-Gate: another crowd of photo-opportunistic nobodies who grab the limelight before either being sent on to jail or up to higher office! *(Beat.)* This hearing is just one more episode in a series that will never end. *(Taking a remote TV channel changer from his pocket.)* You will convene no further, Mr. Chairman.

MIRIAM'S FLOWERS
by Migdalia Cruz

Nando - 30s - New York City - Present
Nando and Delfina mourn the death of their young son, Puli.
Nando visits Puli's grave and tells his son of the responsibilities
of men. As he speaks, the depth of his loss becomes evident.

NANDO: Men have to work. You can't be home all the time when
you're a man. You unnerstan me? *(Pause)* And--and I taught you
the same...When you're the man of the house, you work. I work.
I know you unnerstan. Women don't unnerstan. They expect you
to be there all the time, watching over everything.--I can't be in two
places at the same time, Puli. I know you know that. I'm not no
fuckin' magician. *(Pause)* And it's a good job I have for the kind
of brain I got. I can always remember numbers. That's important
in a post office...I put numbers together in my head and they come
out like a picture. Like the number seven, I see it and it's a big
wooden arrow pointing out. *(Pause)* So...when you got a family,
you make money. You watch out for your sisters. And you don't
let nobody look at your wife. You don't let other men look at
what's yours. You...take care of it. *(Pause)* Men don't get scared.
Not of other men. If you get scared of other men, you hide it. It
helps if you hit them...Yeah, when you feel they bones cracked
against your fist, that's a good feeling. We keep it under control.
My papi used to tell me that the only people you respect are the
people who can beat you...*(He bounces the ball off the gravestone
in silence.)* Puerto Ricans are good at baseball. That's another
thing women don't unnerstan. If you play good baseball, you can be
good at everything else because nothing else means anything...I
wasn't ever really good at it, but my papi wanned me to be. I know
he did because he beat the shit outta me when ever I missed a
catch...He tole me only faggots like carving things outta wood. Men
play sports. And that's right. You don' get nowhere making things.
I mean if you wanned to make things, I woulda let you, but that's
because you got a great arm. When you're good at baseball, people
leave you alone. *(Pause)* People woulda loved you, Puli. You
woulda been something.

MIRIAM'S FLOWERS
by Migdalia Cruz

Nando - 30s - New York City - Present
The grieving Nando visit's Puli's grave and tells a story of a
time that he stepped in ice cream while wearing new shoes.
This eventually turns into an allegory of his love for Delfina.

NANDO: It started with these shoes. They're the first ones I got
that make my feet look like I always thought they should look. Like
I used to think my feet didn't deserve nothing on them. Nothing
good. Because they was so big--like monster feet. Nobody could
love feet like that...So I don't blame her. She keeps me off, but I
don't blame her...but she won't keep me off no more. I know who
I am because when I look down there I can see myself and I like
what I see...sometimes. That's what give me the idea. I was
walking with these fine, hightone shoes and I stepped on a pile of
dogshit. I mean, that's what I thought--so I was standing there
cursing it out, screaming at the street "Hey, fucking street with the
fucking shit on it! I wanna kill you, you fucking street." "Fucking
assholes," I said. "Fucking stupid people with stupid fucking dogs!"
But then, from the bottom of my shoes came this perfume. I hada
close my eyes a minute because it was so sweet...it almost made me
fall over. And then I figured out it was ice cream. Somebody left
this whole pile of ice cream smack in the middle of the street.
Chocolate. Dark. And it had these sticks sticking out of it. Like
a porcupine or something. It was a pile of ice cream pops all melted
together and put out on the street. *(Pause)* I took those sticks home
because they made me think of Fina. She's like a stick for me that
I don't ever wanna be without, like the ones people use when they're
pulling themselves up mountains. Ever since then, everytime I saw
one--in the garbage or on the street, I picked it up and saved it. And
if I passed a candy store, sometimes I'd buy one and eat it real, real,
real slow. I smell like chocolate now. I can see when she sees me
how her nose opens up...those two little holes calling to me...She
really likes chocolate--and with my spit all over it, it's gonna make
her think of me. I'm gonna be inside her all the time now...It's like
magic.

43

NEDDY

by Jeffrey Hatcher

Ned - 30s-40s - Hopkins Hycroft Academy, East Coast Prep School - Present

Ned is the worm that turns in this tale of the caste system within a prep school faculty. Ned is a weakling who collapses when his wife walks out, taking everything with her. A darling among the faculty, he isn't at a loss for company as his friends rally to his support. Allan, for one, loans him $50 and is shocked to discover that he used the money to buy a tie. Ned defends his weakness in the following self-pitying monologue.

NED: Allan. I am a Social Studies teacher. I believe in the inevitability of History. This is my <u>destiny</u>, Allan. Before this happened, the most tragic event I could name was <u>CITIZEN KANE</u> not winning Best Picture in 1941. Now...

[ALLAN: Don't blame yourself, Ned.]

NED: I don't blame myself, I blame Alan Alda. I was a "seventies" kind of guy. I came of age in the "seventies". I was trained to be sensitive. 'Cause I was a "seventies" kind of guy. 'Cause I listened to Alan Alda. Alan Alda and I were going to tear-down male oppression. Alan Alda and I were going to become the "New Men." I never insisted on handling the money. I never insisted on winning a fight. I did the dishes. I read "Our Bodies, Our Selves" and nobody even asked me to. I thought I was safe. I thought I was only doing what Alan Alda would have wanted me to. And now...I'm living in Hemingway's nightmare. I wish my mother had made me take a paper route.

[ALLAN: Ned...]

NED: I am slack, Allan. I am a slack man. Jack Dempsey would have kicked me in the teeth for a lark. Allan. I didn't just buy that tie to cheer me up. I just didn't have anything else I could make into a <u>noose</u>.

[ALLAN: Ned...!]

NED: Don't tell anyone else, Allan. I just felt <u>you</u> should know because I...wanted some <u>pity</u>. I'm better than this, Allan. I am the model of an educated articulate human being, and I am living like a rat in a cage.

NEDDY
by Jeffrey Hatcher

David - 30s-40s - Hopkins Mycroft Academy, East Coast Prep School - Present
Like the proverbial phoenix, Ned is finally to rise from the ashes of his wasted life and proceeds to metamorphose into a veritable dynamo of a handyman. At first his friends are pleased that Ned has taken control of his life, but when his success uncovers their own weaknesses, they begin to resent him. Ned is finally shunned by all of his former friends including David, a chemistry teacher who has been assigned to take over Ned's history classes. David addresses the class on the subject of charity, and the roots of his resentment of Ned become clear.

DAVID: Now, I'm just a Chemistry teacher, so it would be unethical for me to intrude on another's academic field, <u>particularly</u> when substituting in a class on "Problems of Democracy." It <u>would</u> be <u>unethical</u>. But what the hell. *(David turns upstage, and a large Chemistry Table rolls out to meet. Sink, faucet, many beakers filled with red and blue liquids. As he speaks, David dons a lab coat, gloves, and protective goggles over his dinner jacket.)* In all civilized groupings, there is a Ruling Class. And with every Ruling Class, you will encounter a thing called Charity. Now the "primary rationale" for Charity is not "kindness" or "responsibility" or "the improving of weaker lives." The primary rationale for Charity is to <u>keep certain elements in their place</u>--by reminding those elements just who <u>controls</u> the Charity. And if the elements remain distinctly separate--know their place--there is Order. *(David mixes a Blue Liquid with a Red Liquid. The liquids separate.)* But if--instead of firmly wielding Charity--one <u>experiments</u> with the balance of the elements, alters their properties, erases their distinctions, forgets their place...there will be Chaos. *(David mixes a Blue Liquid and a Red Liquid. Smoke erupts from a beaker.)* Or course, for the dispassionate, neutral scientists, there <u>are</u> joys in observing the elements collide into Chaos. After all, what are friends for? And what, you may ask, does all this have to do with "Problems of

45

Democracy"? Some of this school's Future Leaders--and you know who you are--have been observed "helping out" in the cafeteria, "running errands" for the school nurse, and "cleaning chalkboards" after class. Well, we have the guy with the hump for that. You may be well-meaning, but you are in danger of <u>blurring the distinctions</u>. And that's not what you're here for. You're here to learn from our example. In Society--as in Chemistry--certain elements are not meant to mix. Of course, this is not my field of study. This is a dynamic that had to be explained to me. By a particular girlfriend of mine. One who left me recently. Day after Labor Day. At any rate, as I say, it's not my discipline. I'm just a Chemistry teacher.

OH, THE INNOCENTS
by Ari Roth

Jeremy - 20s-30s - New York City - Present
Jeremy is a private music teacher who believes that he is being
seduced by the wealthy (and sexy) mother of one of his students.
Here, he tells Josh, his friend, of a rather sensual fantasy that he
had about this woman while watching his wife sleep.

JEREMY: I thought up some weird shit last night. Betsy sleeping
right next to me like this kitten.
[JOSH: The mother?]
JEREMY: Weird shit.
[JOSH: You whack off to her?]
JEREMY: I just sorta...had this vision.
[JOSH: Any good?]
JEREMY: Betsy sleeping right next to me like this kitten. You
know, like a baby cat.
[JOSH: I KNOW what a kitten is.]
JEREMY: I got like this furry relationship. There's like
WOMBATS out there; people are killing each other two blocks from
where I live; I'm just LYING here. All this light's coming in from
the window; it's summer. It's late. The phone rings. And it's The
Test: Says she's calling from her car phone--costs a dollar-sixty
cents to call; kid tells me this--Says she's going for a drive around
the river. Smoke some dope. No sex. Just a lot of fresh air, she
can't sleep, and I'm thinking, "This woman drives a Lamborghini...
Convertible." Impossible, you say? So do I. At this point, I can't
sleep. I get up, I actually tip-toe down the stairs. And I'm waiting.
(Music) I'm leaning on this fence. The sky is all pink and sort of
pregnant with these clouds. Lightning clouds. She drives up. She
is wearing a paper skirt. It's about as light as a potato print. I open
the door, and she has got these incredibly thin legs. We don't say
a word. We're like those people in some video who don't ever have
to TALK. We start driving 'round the East River and I'm thinking,
"Who is this person? What am I doing?" "Roll the joint," she says,

which is funny, you see, because I smoke the stuff--I mean I'VE SMOKED, I'm not one of these MORALITY HOUNDS--I've just, you know, never actually...rolled. So it's about rolling a joint along the F.D.R. Drive and all these streetlights keep blinking; we're post-something--apocalyptic, maybe pre--the point is, it's empty; it's quiet, and you have never seen anything as peaceful as that road, Josh, and all I want to do is just...attack her! I mean, this feeling I am having is completely foreign. Here I'm sitting in this car, the name of which I can barely PRONOUNCE, with this woman I do not even KNOW; this woman with this MISERABLE LIFE, with these LEGS FROM ANOTHER PLANET; she is sitting right next to me, and all she is doing is...smiling.

ONE-ACT PLAY
by Yannick Murphy

Ray - late teens-20s - Rural America - Present
As a rural family struggles to cope with the desertion of their father, Ray, the oldest son, discovers a place of calm from which he can objectively contemplate their domestic situation.

RAY: I've been there before. Why there's a little house down there with a hole in the front porch, and it's my home. I grew up there. There's a nail on the floor board that catches my sock everytime I walk across it. My mother, occasionally, when she's mad, takes a hammer and beats the nail back down again. But it pops up every winter or so. I know it all down there. On the left, not too far from my house, is a farm. They got watercress growin' down there in the stream now. When I was little their barn got struck by lightnin', a cow was bringin' her calf into the world, and just as the lightnin' struck the mother, the youngun was outta the sack and clear of danger. It's good down there. At 2:10 in the mornin' a train comes by. My Mama says the only time she woke up at 2:10 in the mornin' was when the train didn't come. Delayed a while back durin' a storm. It's home down there. When my Daddy left he gave my mother a 10 pound bag of flour as a going away gift. But he's still in the house. I smelled him in her closet, and Lexy sees him in Mama's eyes. My grandma's dead. When she came to visit, she'd bring her own towel to place on our furniture to sit on, she thought the chairs were infested. Now, still, when I sit down in the easy chair I get itchy. Then I remember why. It's good down there. It's home.

PLAYERS IN A GAME
by Dale Wasserman

The Bishop of Prague - 50s-60s - City of Prague - 1316 A.D.
The complexities of both political and spiritual intrigue of 14th
century Europe are illustrated in this tale of the Bishop of
Prague. As he introduces himself to the audience, we are
treated to a glimpse of his wry humor.

BISHOP: Shall we begin? *(Lights brighten. He regards the
audience benevolently. He speaks to them.)* Beginnings are
difficult. *(He ponders. Declaiming.)* Early in the fourteenth
century the popes of the Catholic Church, having been driven out of
Rome, took refuge in the French town of Avignon. From there they
ruled, giving orders, issuing bulls... *(Sensing disapproval among the
Players.)* Too historical? *(Right. Another approach.)* In the year
1316 the Holy Inquisition set a new mark by burning 3,755 people
at the stake. Or course they were burned for their own good. If any
of them thought otherwise it is not on record. What is on record,
however, is that the ecstatic outcries of those ascending to heaven
rose in an inspiring chorus which...which... *(The Players are
wincing.)* Too hysterical. *(Changing style.)* In the year 1316 the
city of Prague, which is in Bohemia, was a rich and a happy place
to live.
[PLAYERS: *(Approving softly sung.)* Amen...]
BISHOP: Tolerance was the rule, laissez-faire the order of the era.
Minor sins were ignored as a matter of policy...major sins were
almost non-existant. There was little immorality since the city had
very nearly forgotten its definition. Jailers and executioners found
it necessary to seek employment elsewhere. The city hummed in a
harmony of content.
[PLAYERS: *(Sung.)* Amen...]
BISHOP: And all was due to the influence of one extraordinary
man. He was an artist...architect...statesman...prince withour peer.
A man of wit. Eloquence. Compassion. He was Jan the Fourth...
the incomparable Bishop of Prague. Me.

PRELUDE TO A KISS
by Craig Lucas

Old Man - 60s-70s - New York City Area - Present
The soul of a young woman and a dying old man trade places in this unusual love story. As both struggle with their new lives and bodies, they learn that they need desperately to return to their true selves. Here, Rita, the young woman, addresses the audience in the body of the old man.

OLD MAN: You know...if you think how we're born and we go through all the struggle of growing up and learning the multiplication tables and the name for everything, the rules, how not to get run over, braid your hair, pig-Latin. Figuring out how to sneak out of the house late at night. Just all the ins and outs, the _effort_, and learning to accept all the flaws in everybody and everything. And then getting a job, probably something you don't even like doing for not enough money like tending bar, and that's if you're lucky. That's if you're not born in Calcutta or Ecuador or the U.S. without money. Then there's your marriage and raising your own kids if... you know. And they're going through the same struggle all over again, only worse, because somebody's trying to sell them crack in the first grade by now. And all this time you're paying taxes and your hair starts to fall out and you're wearing six pairs of glasses which you can never find and you can't recognize yourself in the mirror and your parents die and your friends, again if you're lucky and it's not you first. And if you live long enough, you finally get to watch everybody die: all your loved ones, your wife, your husband and your kids, maybe, and you're totally alone. And as a final reward for all this...you disappear. _(Pause.)_ No one knows where. _(Pause.)_ So we might as well have a good time while we're here, don't you think?

THE PUPPETMASTER OF LODZ
by Gilles Ségal
translated by Sara O'Connor

Finkelbaum - 30s-50s - Outskirts of Berlin - 1950
Finkelbaum is a survivor of Birkenau living in Berlin in 1950.
His experiences in the concentration camp, including the death
of his wife have driven him to the edge of madness. When a
friend from the camp finds him, he helps to pull him back to
reality. Finkelbaum is finally ready to face the memory of
finding his wife in a pile of bodies to be burned. As he tells his
friend this dreadful memory, healing finally begins.

FINKELBAUM: You know what's marvellous about you? You say
to yourself: this poor Finkelbaum has gone mad, but you don't say:
let's also play mad to bring him along, no, you push friendship to
the point of wanting to really become mad! One can't imagine a
better friend than you...But's it's not enough to want to,
Schweinkopf...otherwise I would have gone mad a long time ago...
Lord knows, I've tried...tried with all my might but...you see when
I found Ruchele, that October day...in the pile of corpses we had to
burn, I thought I was going to go mad...Ruchele with our child in
her belly...but I didn't rip open my chest to tear the heart out... I
continued to...and later I even followed you to run away...in order
to live! You see, for me, not to have become mad, that it the most
shattering proof of the non-existence of God...Since then, I try, I
try...Sometimes I say to myself, that's it...I touch it with my finger
and pfft...it boils down to an idea for the production I'll never
mount...a little imagination, yes...madness, no...But the war...that,
yes...if I had succeeded in truly believing that it wasn't over...I
would perhaps have been able...but no, you had to come...to save
me again!...It was me who stole your bread...and you, poor
schmuck, you brought me more...

PVT. WARS
by James McLure

Silvio - 20s-30s - VA Hospital - Present
Silvio is a street-smart vet struggling to cope with life in a VA
Hospital. His good-humored propensity to flash the nursing staff
has earned him quite a reputation among the staff and his fellow
vets. In a session with the hospital psychiatrist, Silvio reveals,
among other things, his love for his mother.

SILVIO: I don't know. I have these strange thoughts. They're not
violent. *(Pause.)* Some of them are violent. The other day I, uhm,
was talking to this old woman. And she was talking and I just
wanted to do some outrageous thing to her. Like slap her. Or pull
her false teeth out. Or play with the flab on her face. I mean, I
wouldn't but--it's something I think about. *(Pause.)* When I was
little I used to think I could talk to God. In fact, I thought I could
talk to God better than anybody in the world and I didn't understand
why world leaders didn't come to me to pray to God to solve the
world's problems. I'd sit in church with my family. And my
mother--my mother is a very beautiful woman. She looks like Italian
women on jars of spaghetti sauce. And she's got big old bosoms.
And I like 'em. And I don't care what that sounds like 'cause it's
one of my favorite parts of my mother. *(Pause.)* And I remember
when my father died, it, uh, she showed great dignity. She took my
hand and she said, "You go take care of your sister now." And I
said, "Who's gonna take care of you?" And she said, "I can take
care of myself, you take care of your sister." And I said, "But I
want to take care of you?" And she said, "Look, you get in there
and take care of your sister before I knock you into the middle of
next week." And I did. And my sister was so pretty when she--was
in her confirmation dress. *(Pause.)* Somebody's been flashing the
nurses? I don't know anything about that. It wasn't me. *(Pause.)*
It wasn't me.

PVT. WARS
by James McLure

Natwick - 20s-30s - VA Hospital - Present
Natwick feels as though he has failed at life. When his friends
go out for a night on the town without him, his feelings of
uselessness and alienation drive him to the contemplation of
suicide.

NATWICK: Great. They've gone out on a date. They didn't even
invite me. They're my best friends and even they hate me. They
hate me. They hate me almost as much as I hate them. "I should
have been a pair of ragged claws scuffling across the floors of silent
seas." Say. That's good...*(Realization.)* Of course, it's good,
asshole. That's T.S. Eliot. *(He pulls the tie very sharply around his
neck. He ties the other end around the neck of chair. He tosses
chair over. It jerks him over. Inspects tie/chair.)* Of course. This
is the way to pull teeth, not kill yourself. Let's get serious. *(He
gets up. He takes out a piece of paper. Reads.)* Isn't anything I
write original? *(Reading from paper.)*
"I dare not meet your eyes in dreams.
For love is not the song it seems.
The breach between what seems and means
comes to us only in our dreams."
They'll appreciate me when I'm gone. *(He takes a bottle of pills
from his pocket.)* Barbituates. There's the ticket. Good 'ol
barbituates and alcohol. Great death. The death most often selected
by celebrities. Sure. Won't feel a thing. *(He swallows the pills.
Washes it down with alcohol.)* Won't be long now...soon will be
dead...that's a depressing thought. Natwick. You are a loathsome
individual. No, I'm not. I am an invention of myself. A stillbirth
who lived and gave birth to himself. And I lived. *(Pause.)* There's
never anyone to dance with. *(He dances alone. Elegantly,
gracefully.)*

QUEEN OF THE LEAKY ROOF CIRCUIT
by Jimmy Breslin

Eugene - 30s-40s - New York City - Present

Poverty has often led Eugene to commit petty crimes in order to stay alive. Here, he tells his friends of the time he was almost recruited to play college basketball.

EUGENE: Reginald, you make me remember the first time a man said I could have a car.

[BEATRICE: Who gave you a car?]

EUGENE: That was when people were trying to give me everything. I had a shot from the corner that I learned in the Livonia Avenue park. The rim was so loose nobody could even make a layup. Didn't bother me. I jus' put the ball right through the hole, touched nothing. They heard about my shot from here to California. Man takes me to Tu-lane college, down New Orleans. I didn't graduate from Thomas Jefferson, but they say to me, don' worry, your big test at Tu-lane is foul line. The Tu-lane coach shows me this brand new Trans Am right in front of the school president's house, big old white house. I go, wow. The coach says, don' drive off yet. Come in the gym and shoot a few baskets. I go inside. The coach have nine other guys there. They all like me. Down from high schools. The coach starts us off in a regular full court game. Now I got this real nice shot, y' understand. I just roll it off my fingers nice, and I see the basket nice and the first time I get the ball, I start to roll my shot off. Here come this hand up there. Just up there enough so I shoot this little bit over it. Miss my main shot. Ever time I be aimin' my shot, this hand come up there in the air. The dude guardin' me, he didn't look nothin', all bones, and I say, "What are you?" He look down at me. "Six foot eight." Playin' backcourt. Six eight. After the game, the coach says to me, "You about five inches from bein' a great player. You got your carfare home all right?" I say to him, "I'm goin' to drive home in that Trans Am." The coach say, "That Trans Am now belong to the boy guardin' you. He stayin' here. You goin' home." Sure did go home. Come home to Brooklyn and got myself a car. I stole it right in front of a man's house in Bay Ridge. *(He hands Reginald the car back.)*

REBEL ARMIES DEEP INTO CHAD
by Mark Lee

Dove - 50s - Northern Nairobi - Present
Dove is a British journalist stationed in Nairobi. He has spent his entire life trying to separate himself from the drama of daily events, and the effort has left him bitter. When Neal, a young American journalist, turns up at his door with tales of brutality in Uganda, Dove reacts with frustration. Here, he blames his destruction on Africa.

DOVE: I'm calling the police! We've had an attempted robbery here! An assault with a knife and... *(Silence. The women are frightened. A beat, then Dove hangs up. He hesitates, then picks up the empty bottles from the coffee table.)* You see before you another victim of a classical education. *(Dove drops the bottles into the trash. He picks up the wash bowl left on the coffee table and places it in the sink.)* I should have studied the Sciences or stayed away from college all together, but no...I had read Tactitus and his fellow historians. I admired them. I really did. Their elevated tone. Their calm voices describing scenes of human frailty. They were always...above it all. And that's the way I wanted to be...above it all. For awhile, it was all quite possible. I was well on the road to becoming a Senior Editor...one of those men who interviews heads of state and writes about the "big picture" for the Sunday supplements. Then, they sent me to Africa "for seasoning." Good God. As if I was a piece of meat that needed a little more salt. *(He walks over to the writing table.)* So, I came here and stayed and stayed and you destroyed me. Not you two personally of course, but the whole bloody continent. I didn't believe in the big picture anymore. It was a lie. A total illusion.

REBEL ARMIES DEEP INTO CHAD
by Mark Lee

Dove - 50s - Northern Nairobi - Present
When Neal accuses Dove of not caring about anything, he
responds with passion about the numbing consequences of being
presented with starvation and poverty on a daily basis.

DOVE: And who am I supposed to care about? Every beggar on
the street? Do you have any idea of what I've seen and walked
away from in my life? Children...sick and starving with sunken eyes
and rust-red hair coming off in patches from their skin. A woman
shivering with malaria...dying for want of a grain of quinine. A
man in Ethiopia about to be shot...his hands tied, his eyes pleading
to me as if I could save him. And those are just the things I've
seen. What about the daily dose of death and disaster that spews out
of the telex? We have too much news today. Too much to really
care. What can I do about the situation? What can anyone do but
walk outside and howl at the moon?

SANTIAGO
by Manuel Pereiras

Husband - 42 - Santiago - Present
In this absurdist look at the perils of daily life in Santiago, the
Husband is a vicious torturer, employed by the government to
ferret out "confessions" from enemies of the state. He revels in
his work, as can be seen in this monologue in which he defends
his vocation to his wife by comparing his killing to her choice
to abort their children.

HUSBAND: *(Facing her)* Listen to her! What about your
abortions? You've had many abortions.
[SHE: It's not the same.]
HUSBAND: It's the same. When does a fetus get his brain? The
last fetus you aborted had hair. You could see the veins in his head.
You destroy them because they invade your body. Those I kill
invade my territory. All I stand for. You should understand why
I kill those bastards. That's what they are--fucking bastard queers.
They don't belong here. What's the difference?
[SHE: I read somewhere...]
HUSBAND: Don't tell me what you read. My killing those
bastards is no different from your killing those little buggers who get
inside you. I enjoy it as much as you enjoy it. I get the hanger. I
untwist it right before their eyes. They don't know what it's for.
Most think I'm going to put it up their asses. A hot iron up your ass
is a big discomfort. We used to do it--put a hot iron up their asses.
But not any more. It's a new policy. No hangers up their asses.
Now, we pull their eyes out with the hangers. I stand behind them.
(He walks behind the chair where She sits.) They start looking
sideways, like this. *(He moves her face to the side; mimics what
he's describing.)* I pop that very eye out. It's easy. I've mastered
the stroke. It's impressive: the way that white and red ball comes
out. Sometimes, it seems to be staring at you from the floor. The
queers never see it; they faint immediately. *(He walks left.)*
Tongue-pulling makes them faint even faster. That's the first thing

58

SANTIAGO

I cut out. Tongues. Images leave my mind; sounds stick in my brain. Their screams gave me a few bad dreams. Not nightmares. I never have nightmares. I get rid of their tongues first thing-- tongues and all that comes with them. They faint like daisies. We have to revive them and cut their organs one by one. The fingers, the teeth. Those are not really organs, eh? It's a steady job. We've never been hungry. I'm not cruel. I'd rather kill them than pull their eyes or their teeth out. I'd rather kill them than cut their tongues or their fingers. But they have to pay; they have to feel they're paying. We have to cut them into pieces. The final touch is the cutting of their cocks.

SARA

by Gotthold Ephraim Lessing

translated by Ernest Bell

Sir William - 50s - England - 1755

Sir William has followed Sara, his beloved daughter, and her
lover to an inn. He sends his servant to her with a letter in
which he forgives them both. When the servant returns with the
news that Sara still loves him, he rejoices.

SIR WILLIAM: What balm you have poured on my wounded heart
with your words, Waitwell! I live again, and the prospect of her
return seems to carry me as far back to my youth as her flight had
brought me nearer to my grave. She loves me still? What more do
I wish! Go back to her soon, Waitwell! I am impatient for the
moment when I shall fold her again in these arms, which I had
stretched out so longingly to death! How welcome would it have
been to me in the moments of my grief! And how terrible will it be
to me in my new happiness! And old man, no doubt, is to be
blamed for drawing the bonds so tight again which still unite him to
the world. The final separation becomes the more painful. But God
who shows Himself so merciful to me now, will also help me to go
through this. Would he, I ask, grant me a mercy in order to let it
become my ruin in the end? Would He give me back a daughter,
that I should have to murmur when He calls me from life? No, no!
He gives her back to me that in my last hour I may be anxious about
myself alone. Thanks to Thee, Eternal Father! How feeble is the
gratitude of mortal lips! But soon, soon I shall be able to thank Him
more worthily in an eternity devoted to Him alone!

SARA

by Gotthold Ephraim Lessing

translated by Ernest Bell

Mellefont - 30s - England - 1755
Mellefont, a selfish rake, here considers the possibility of marriage with his beloved Sara. This is the first time that he has truly been in love, and yet he cannot bring himself to commit to the idea of marriage.

MELLEFONT: *(After walking up and down several times in thought.)* What a riddle I am to myself! What shall I think myself? A fool? Or a knave? Heart, what a villain thou art! I love the angel, however much of a devil I may be. I love her! Yes, certainly! Certainly I love her. I feel I would sacrifice a thousand lives for her, for her who sacrificed her virtue for me; I would do so--this very moment without hesitation would I do so. And yet, yet--I am afraid to say it to myself--and yet--how shall I explain it? And yet I fear the moment which will make her mine for ever before the world. It cannot be avoided now, for her father is reconciled. Nor shall I be able to put it off for long. The delay has already drawn down painful reproaches enough upon me. But painful as they were, they were still more supportable to me than the melancholy thought of being fettered for life. But am I not so already? Certainly--and with pleasure! Certainly I am already her prisoner. What is it I want, then? At present I am a prisoner, who is allowed to go about on parole; that is flattering! Why cannot the matter rest there? Why must I be put in chains and thus lack even the pitiable shadow of freedom? In chains? Quite so! Sara Sampson, my beloved! What bliss lies in these words! Sara Sampson, my wife! The half of the bliss is gone! And the other half--will go! Monster that I am! And with such thoughts shall I write to her father? Yet these are not my real thoughts, they are fancies! Cursed fancies, which have become natural to me through my dissolute life! I will free myself from them, or live no more.

SCAREFIELD
by Louis Phillips

Crow - Any Age - Any Time - Any Place
An outspoken crow explains the symbiotic nature of his relationship with the scarecrow in this absurdist retelling of The Wizard of Oz.

CROW: Don't take offense. You and I are locked together in this enterprise like ham and eggs, alternating and current, Getrude and Hamlet, Heaven and Hell. Why are we linked together? I'll tell you why. Because voids of our Father flock together. Like scared and sacred. Ever notice how similar those two words are--scared and sacred. Just a simple juxtaposition and that which is frightened and humiliated turns into something associated with the godhead. And you think all you've got to do is stand around in the middle of nowhere and think. Nothing you ever thought of that crow didn't think of first. Nothing. So don't you worry, buddy. I'm going to make you and your friend look so good that they won't need another scarecrow in this place for another million years. The cretaceous, jurassic, triassic, permian, pennsylvanian, mississippian, devonian, silurian, ordovician, cambrian, pre-cambrian will have come and gone like so much spit in God's eye. There's nothing more for you to think about.

SEARCH AND DESTROY
by Howard Korder

Ron - 30s-50s - New York City - Present
Martin is desperate to raise money for a film project and is
determined to do anything to get what he wants--including
selling drugs. His search for cash takes him to New York City,
where he is introduced to Ron, a desperate character who hides
his drug dealing behind a guise of selling landscaping equipment.
Here Ron tells Martin why he loves New York.

RON: Miami. Miami. Fucking Miami. Fucking skeeve town.
Fucking Cubans. Crazed fucking mothers. I hate fucking Miami.
You're not safe in Miami. How the fuck you live there I don't
know.
[KIM: Martin doesn't live in Miami, Ron.]
[RON: He doesn't?]
[MARTIN: No.]
[RON: Where the fuck *does* he live?]
[MARTIN: Boca Raton.]
[RON: Huh. Well. *You* go down there, huh? Kim? You go down
Miami, right?]
[KIM: I sometimes go to Miami.]
RON: You're fucking *crazy. New* York. *New* York. *New* York.
Last night?
[KIM: How was it?]
RON: The best. The best. Absofuckingwhatly the best. Last
night. Okay. We get there. This is at Shea. We get there. In the
limo. I got, I'm with, the, *Carol,* she does the, the, *fuck,* you
know, that *ad,* the fitness, amazing bod, amazing bod, fucking
amazing bod, and I have, for this occasion, I put aside my very best,
lovely lovely blow, for Carol, who, no, I care about very deeply.
So, okay, get to Shea, it's fucking *bat* night, everybody with the
bats, fifty thousand bat-wielding sociopaths, security is very tight.
I have a private booth. In the circle. This is through GE, my little
addictive exec at GE. So we entree, me and Carol, and my client,

63

I see, has fucked me over, 'cause there's already someone there, you know who, that talk-show guy, he's always got like three drag queens and a Satanist, and he's there with a girl can't be more than fourteen. "Oops." This fucking guy, my *daughter* watches that show. And between us, heavy substance abuser. I ask him to leave. I mean I come to watch a ball game with my good friend Carol and I'm forced to encounter skeevy baby-fucking cokeheads. One thing leads to the other, politeness out the window he comes at me Mets ashtray in his hand. What do I do.

[KIM: You have a bat.]

RON: I have a bat, I take this bat, I acquaint this individual in the head with this bat. "Badoing." Right, badoing? He doesn't go down. Stands there, walks out the door, comes back two security guards. "Is there a problem here, boys?" "Well sir, this man, bicka bicka bicka." "Yes, I completely understand and here's something for your troubles."

[KIM: How much?]

RON: How much, Kim? How much did I give these good men to resolve our altercation? I gave them one thousand dollars in U.S. currency. And they were very grateful. Mr. Microphone sits down, doesn't speak, doesn't move rest of the night. Moody fucking person. Mets take it, great ball, home with Carol where we romp in the flower of our youth. I win. I dominate. I get all the marbles. And that is why I love New York.

SEX, DRUGS, ROCK & ROLL
by Eric Bogosian

X-Blow - 20s - New York City - Present
A home-boy ex-con considers Ronald Reagan, power and
Batman in this rap-style stream of urban consciousness. The
young man reveals the fact that he has killed and that it felt
good.

X-BLOW: I'm a child of nature, born to lose,
people call me "Poison" but that's no news.
When I wake up in the morning, I see what I see,
I look into the mirror, what I see is me:
A player, a winner, a unrepentant sinner -
if you mess with me, I'll eat you for dinner.
There are those that rule and those that serve,
I'm the boss baby cause I got the nerve
to take what I want, take what I need
cut you first sucker and make you bleed.
Cause life's a bitch, that I know.
Don't misunderstand me or then you'll go
to your grave in a rocket, nothing in your pocket,
if you got a gun, you better not cock it,
cause then you'll die, that I know
the rest of you away will blow
and you will spend eternity
praying to God you never met me!

He dissed my ass, he dissed my ass! I had no choice.
    I walked up to him, I stuck my screwdriver into his stomach
and I ran it right true his heart. He looked surprized man. Skinny
kid like me, killing him like dat. Hah. Didn't even bleed.
    Felt good man, felt better than gettin' laid on a sunny day.
And I like to feel good, know what I'm saying? Feeling good makes
me feel good. Don't need no sucker drugs to feel good.
    'Fore they locked me up I used to get up every morning and

65

SEX, DRUGS, ROCK & ROLL

I had me two problems, how to find money and how to spend it. All the rest was gravy. Like the guy says, "Don't worry, be happy."

But you know that was the Reagan years and the Reagan years is over man and I miss 'em! Ronnie Reagan, he was my main man. He had that cowboys and Indians shit down solid. But now he's out in LA sitting on a horse and we're sitting in the shit he left behind. But it's OK, he's gone. Now a new man's in charge! BATMAN! Batman is my man!

We gonna fly now, get into outer space like Kirk and Scotty, like the Jetsons man! Just beaming around, beaming around. Be fine! Jump into my Batmobile, get behind some smoked bullet-proof windshield, pop in the CD and flip the dial to ten, rock the engine, burn the brakes...man that's living...You can smoke that shit! You only live once, you gotta grab that gusto shit.

ZOYA'S APARTMENT
by Mikhail Bulgakov
translated by Nicholas Saunders
and Frank Dwyer

Aleksander Tarasovich Ametistov - 30s-40s - Moscow - 1922
Aleksander Tarasovich Ametistov is a man forced to survive by
his wits since the Russian Revolution of 1917. In 1922, he
appears, penniless, at his cousin Zoya's Moscow apartment
seeking a place to live. Here, he tells Zoya the complex tale of
his adventures and misadventures since the Revolution in hopes
of being invited to stay.

AMETISTOV: But here comes the White Army, so the Reds give
me money to evacuate to Moscow. But I take off for Rostov,
instead, and go to work for the Whites...Here come the Reds!...So
the Whites give me money to evacuate, but I go back to the Reds
instead and become the Chief of their Political Agitation Corps...
Here come the Whites again!...So the Reds come up with my
Evacuation Expenses, and I head for the Whites in Crimea. I find
work as the manager of a little restaurant in Sevastopol, where I get
involved in a friendly game of chemin de fer and drop 300,000
rubles in a single night...
[ZOYA: Really? They must have been experts.]
AMETISTOV: Savages, I'm telling you, degenerates, a real bunch
of thieves!...Oh, well, you know the rest...more Whites, more Reds,
and I began to bounce around the whole Soviet system. In
Stavropol, I was an actor. In Novocherkask, a musician in the Fire
Department. In Voronezh, I was put in charge of the Food Supply...
My career was no longer advancing, I had to admit it...so I decided
it was time to reach out for the Party line. To tell you the truth, I
almost didn't make it. How could I cut through the bureaucracy and
acquire the necessary credentials, how, how...? when all of a
sudden a friend of mine named Chemodanov died in my room...
What a happy-go-lucky man he was, Karl Petrovich...and a Party
Member, too...

ZOYA'S APARTMENT

[ZOYA: This was in Varonezh?]

AMETISTOV: No, I'm in Odessa now. Why should the Party be the loser, I thought. One man falls, another takes his place, like legionnaires. So I shed a few tears over the corpse, lifted his Party Card, and set off for Baku. Here's a sleepy little oil town, I thought, I can start up a chemin de fer game and set this place on fire. So I go around and introduce myself as Chemodanov. And the next thing you know--boom!--my door flies open. It's a friend of Chemodanov's! What a scene!! He's got nine and I've got nothing! I head for the window...but we're not on the ground floor.

[ZOYA: What a story!]

AMETISTOV: A little bad luck, Zoyechka, what can you do? I didn't draw the card I needed...but I made such an eloquent summation at the trial that even my guards were sobbing!...So they shot me...What next? When a man loses everything, it's time to go to Moscow. And now I'm here, where's the Zoyka I used to know? You've grown callous, sitting here in your apartment...you've cut yourself off from the masses!

ZOYA'S APARTMENT
by Mikhail Bulgakov
translated by Nicholas Saunders
and Frank Dwyer

Ametistov - 30s-40s - Moscow - 1922
Ametistov comes to Boris, the money-man and power broker to
further his scheme. When he finds Boris dead and robbed he
knows that his luck has run out in Moscow. He regretfully
prepares to set out for yet another new beginning.

AMETISTOV: *(entering quietly)* Boris Semyonovich, *pardon,*
pardon. Are you resting? Go ahead, rest, rest. How come he left
you by yourself? It's easy to smoke too much when you're not used
to it. What a painful ordeal you've been through. Why, even your
hand is cold... *(He looks more closely.)* Wait a minute! Son of a
bitch!...Murdered! This was not a part of the program, citizens!
Now what?...Finished!...Cherubim!! He plucked him and took off...
Oh, I'm such an idiot!...There goes Nice! There goes Monte Carlo!
(pause; then, lethargically) "The stars are shimmering with light..."
What am I doing? Why am I standing here? Onward! *(He tears off*
his coat and tie, runs into Zoya's bedroom, opens the desk drawer,
removes some papers and banknotes and puts them in his pocket,
gets his old suitcase from under the bed, takes out his old jacket and
cap and puts them on.) My faithful companion, my dear old bag,
we're on our own again. But where are we off to? Tell me, dear
comrades, where shall we go? Oh, my star, my cold, indifferent
star!...Oh, my destiny!...Goodbye, Zoya, forgive me! There was
nothing else I could do! Farewell, Zoya's apartment! *(He*
disappears with his suitcase.)

PERMISSIONS ACKNOWLEDGMENTS

Grateful acknowledgment is made for permission to reprint excerpts from the following plays:

AMULETS AGAINST THE DRAGON FORCES by Paul Zindel. Copyright © 1989 by Paul Zindel. Reprinted by permission of the author's agent, Wiley Hausam, International Creative Management, Inc., 40 West 57th Street, New York, NY 10019. Published by Dramatists Play Service, Inc.

APPLES by Ian Dury. Copyright © 1989 by Ian Dury. Reprinted by permission of Faber and Faber, Ltd., 3 Queens Square, London WC1N 3AU, England.

A QUIET END by Robin Swados. Copyright © 1990 by Robin Swados. Reprinted by permission of the author and Graham Agency. CAUTION: Professionals and amateurs are hereby warned that A QUIET END is subject to a royalty. It is fully protected under the copyright laws of the United States of America, and of all countries covered by the International Copyright Union (including Canada and the rest of the British Commonwealth), and of all countries covered by the Pan-American Copyright convention and the Universal Copyright Convention, and of all countries with which the United States has reciprocal copyright relations. All rights, including professional, amateur, motion picture, recitation, lecturing, public reading, radio broadcasting, television, audio and video recording, and the rights of translation into foreign languages are strictly reserved. All inquiries concerning rights should be addressed to Graham Agency, 311 West 43rd Street, New York, New York 10036.

A SILENT THUNDER by Eduardo Ivan Lopez. Copyright © 1985 by Eduardo Ivan Lopez. Reprinted by permission of the author.

AT THE STILL POINT by Jordan Roberts. Copyright © 1990 by Jordan Roberts. Reprinted by permission of the author. AT THE STILL POINT was first produced by: PRIMARY STAGES, New York, Casey Childs, Artistic Director, at the William Redfield Theater, April, 1990.

AUGUST SNOW by Reynolds Price. Copyright © 1989 by Reynolds Price. Reprinted by permission of the author's agent, Harriet Wasserman, 137 East 36th Street, New York, NY 10016.

BRILLIANT TRACES by Cindy Lou Johnson. Copyright © 1989 by Cindy Lou Johnson. Reprinted by permission of the author's agent, George P. Lane, William Morris Agency, 1350 Avenue of the Americas, New York, NY 10019. Published by Dramatists Play Service, Inc.

CANTORIAL by Ira Levin. Copyright © 1990 by Ira Levin. Reprinted by permission of the author's agent, Howard Rosenstone, Rosenstone/Wender, 3 East 48th Street, New York, NY 10017. Published by Samuel French, Inc.

70

71